Military History Chronicles

Also from Westphalia Press
westphaliapress.org

Making an Impact on Thought Leadership and Scholarship

The Journals of American Public University System

American Public University System (APUS) inspires scholars across the globe through its collection of peer-reviewed journals:

- Space Education and Strategic Applications
- Global Security and Intelligence Studies
- International Journal of Open Educational Resources
- Journal of Online Learning Research and Practice
- Saber and Scroll Historical Journal

A pioneer in online higher education, APUS—through American Military University and American Public University—ensures that working professionals are provided the opportunity to take full advantage of a quality affordable education.

Delve into our wide-ranging selection of journals and you'll understand why 200,000+ students and alumni have chosen APUS to help them achieve their scholastic objectives.

APUS—Defining Educational Foundations

Learn more at apus.edu/journals

Military History Chronicles
Volume 1, Number 2 • Winter 2024 Campaign

Westphalia Press
An imprint of Policy Studies Organization
1367 Connecticut Ave NW
Washington, D.C. 20036
info@ipsonet.org

ISBN: 978-1-63723-511-9

Cover and interior design by Jeffrey Barnes
jbarnesbook.design

Daniel Gutierrez-Sandoval, Executive Director
PSO and Westphalia Press

Updated material and comments on this edition
can be found at the Westphalia Press website:
www.westphaliapress.org

MILITARY HISTORY CHRONICLES

Volume 1, Number 2 • Winter 2024 Campaign

Jeffrey Ballard, Editor-in-Chief

Westphalia Press

An imprint of Policy Studies Organization

On the title page: "LVT-1 Boneyard at Tetere Beach." One-hundred and fifty yards inland from the Sealark Channel, near the village of Ghorambau on the South Pacific island of Guadalcanal, is the "World War Two Museum at Tetere Beach." It is not a typical museum by Western standards. There are no walls, no gift shop, and no ticket window. I don't remember seeing a gate or fence, just the sign. A pleasant, smiling man, teeth stained red from chewing betel nut, appeared out of nowhere to collect $100 Solomon (about $12 US) from each of us. Parked in the field to the north and between the giant trees on either side of our van were approximately thirty armored vehicles alternately baked in the tropical sun and rusted into oblivion by the salt air. This vehicle park is the final resting place of the LVT-1s (Landing Vehicle Tracked-1, but popularly known as "Alligators") belonging to the 3rd Amphibian Tractor Battalion. These particular vehicles did not land the First Marine Division on Guadalcanal, whose eighty-first anniversary we were on the island to commemorate. Instead, the 3rdAABn exercised the Third Marine Division in ship-to-shore movements before participating in Operation CARTWHEEL, landing on Bougainville Island on November 1, 1943. Eventually replaced by more powerful and heavily armed models, the tracks were abandoned here on Tetere Beach. Some are lined in rows of twos and threes. Others are haphazardly parked. The jungle consumed those parked too near to its edge. Still, others have burst open as giant banyan trees split them apart from within. The few parked in the kunai grass, all removable parts scrapped by the villagers, are rusted but otherwise recognizable after eight decades. At their current rate of decay, the Gators will still be standing watch over Tetere a thousand years from now. [Used with the permission of J. Ballard]

Military History Chronicles
Volume 1, Number 2 • *Winter 2024 Campaign*
© 2024 Policy Studies Organization

TABLE OF CONTENTS

Dispatch No. 2

While putting together the Winter Campaign's Table of Contents, I realized this issue is skewed towards World War II. This was unintentional but not surprising. Anyone who knows me will tell you that World War II, especially naval history, is my thing. My enthusiasm started with one book: *The Struggle for Guadalcanal*, Volume V of Samuel Eliot Morison's chronicle of the United States Navy in World War II. Since age fourteen, I have dreamed, schemed, and planned to travel to the South Pacific.

On August 10th of this year, I returned home after a twelve-day battlefields tour of Guadalcanal and Tulagi, a trip forty-four years in the making. Ours was more of an expedition than a tour. Col. Joe Mueller USMC (Ret.), our guide, modeled each day on the "staff ride" concept. After breakfast and saluting the American flag, we were gone. "Off like a herd of turtles," to be precise.

More often than not, we started the day at one of the high places on the island—the American War Memorial (Hill 72), Edson's Ridge, or the "Gifu" (Hill 27). With a view of a portion of the First Marine Division 1942 perimeter, we conducted map exercises and planned the daily OP.

Ours was no motorcoach tour ending at the visitor center gift shop. With a bird's eye view of the battlefields in mind, we hiked the ridges and valley trails and breached the dense jungle with machete-wielding locals. Our objective was always to walk the terrain, trudge the mud, and view the battlefield from as many vantage points as possible.

The trip exceeded my expectations tenfold. Six months later, I'm just beginning to process the things that I did and saw on Guadalcanal. The experiences I shared with my Detachment, the images that decades of study conjured in my mind, and the emotions the images uncovered are too vast to tell here. I suspect it will take the rest of my life to express them all adequately.

I have one observation—one that I believe is true for all military historians regardless of your particular interest. You cannot know until you go! Research and map study are no substitute for walking the battlefield. After decades of studying the Guadalcanal Campaign, I thought I knew everything. I thought I knew how steep the slopes of Mt. Austen were. I thought I knew how wide the Lunga River was. I thought Savo Island was farther away and Tulagi was closer. I thought I knew what it was like to walk in razor-sharp kunai grass. I thought I knew how oppressive the heat and humidity were. I was wrong on all accounts. Add exhaustion from months of sustained combat, thirst, starvation, disease, rot, and mosquitoes—my understanding is not even in the same ballpark as the reality of war

 doi: 10.18278/mhc.1.2.1

in the South Pacific in 1942. Oh, and did I mention nobody was trying to kill us?

Wherever your study of history takes you, go! You cannot truly know until you do.

Jeff Ballard

Huntington Beach, California

December 22, 2023

Military History Tours Detachment 23-A1A, near the GSgt. John Basilone (USMC) Medal of Honor position, Guadalcanal Province, Solomon Islands, August 4, 2023. Team: R. Bochman (front). J. Mueller, D. Mosis, J. Ballard, W. Lawson, D. Rumple, and D. McVey (l-r). P. Fetterman (not present). [Used with the permission of J. Ballard]

Comunicado No. 2

Mientras elaboraba el índice de la campaña de invierno, me di cuenta de que este tema está sesgado hacia la Segunda Guerra Mundial. Esto fue involuntario, pero no sorprendente. Cualquiera que me conozca le dirá que lo mío es la Segunda Guerra Mundial, especialmente la historia naval. Mi entusiasmo comenzó con un libro: *La lucha por Guadalcanal, volumen V* de la crónica de Samuel Eliot Morison sobre la Armada de los Estados Unidos en la Segunda Guerra Mundial. Desde los catorce años he soñado, planeado y planificado viajar al Pacífico Sur.

El 10 de agosto de este año regresé a casa después de una gira de doce días por los campos de batalla de Guadalcanal y Tulagi, un viaje que había durado cuarenta y cuatro años. La nuestra fue más una expedición que una gira. El coronel Joe Mueller USMC (retirado), nuestro guía, modeló cada día el concepto de "viaje del personal". Después de desayunar y saludar a la bandera estadounidense, nos fuimos. "Fuera como una manada de tortugas", para ser precisos.

La mayoría de las veces, comenzamos el día en uno de los lugares altos de la isla: el American War Memorial (colina 72), Edson's Ridge o el "Gifu" (colina 27). Con vistas a una parte del perímetro de la Primera División de Infantería de Marina de 1942, realizamos ejercicios cartográficos y planificamos la operación del día.

El nuestro no fue un recorrido en autobús que terminara en la tienda de regalos del centro de visitantes. Con una vista panorámica de los campos de batalla en mente, caminamos por las crestas y senderos del valle y atravesamos la densa jungla con lugareños armados con machetes. Nuestro objetivo siempre fue caminar por el terreno, caminar penosamente por el barro y ver el campo de batalla desde tantos puntos estratégicos como fuera posible.

El viaje superó diez veces mis expectativas. Seis meses después, apenas estoy empezando a procesar las cosas que hice y vi en Guadalcanal. Las experiencias que compartí con mi Destacamento, las imágenes que décadas de estudio evocaron en mi mente y las emociones que revelaron las imágenes son demasiado vastas para contarlas aquí. Sospecho que me tomará el resto de mi vida expresarlos todos adecuadamente.

Tengo una observación, una que creo que es cierta para todos los historiadores militares, independientemente de su interés particular. ¡No puedes saberlo hasta que te vayas! La investigación y el estudio de mapas no sustituyen a caminar por el campo de batalla. Después de décadas de estudiar la Campaña de Guadalcanal, pensé que lo sabía todo. Pensé que sabía lo empinadas que eran las laderas del monte Austen. Pensé que sabía lo ancho que era el río Lunga. Pensé que la isla Savo estaba más lejos y Tulagi más cerca. Pensé que sabía lo que era caminar sobre la afilada hierba kunai. Pensé que sabía lo opresivos que eran el calor y la humedad.

Me equivoqué en todos los aspectos. Si a eso le sumamos el agotamiento por meses de combate sostenido, la sed, el hambre, las enfermedades, la putrefacción y los mosquitos, mi entendimiento ni siquiera está en el mismo estadio que la realidad de la guerra en el Pacífico Sur en 1942. Ah, ¿y mencioné que nadie estaba tratando de matarnos?

Dondequiera que te lleve tu estudio de la historia, ¡ve! No puedes saberlo verdaderamente hasta que lo hagas.

Jeff Ballard

Huntington Beach, California

22 de diciembre de 2023

编者按（第二封电讯）

在整理本期冬季内容目录时，我意识到本期主题聚焦于第二次世界大战。这并非有意安排，但却并不奇怪。认识我的人都会告诉你，二战，尤其是海军历史，是我的专长。我对海军史的热情始于一本书，即塞缪尔·艾略特·莫里森撰写的二战美国海军编年史第五卷《争夺瓜达尔卡纳尔岛》。从十四岁起，我就梦想并计划去南太平洋旅行。

这场旅行在44年后终于得以实现——今年8月10日，我结束了在瓜达尔卡纳尔岛和图拉吉岛度过的为期12天的战场之旅，回到了家。这次旅行更像是一次探险而不是旅行。我们的导游Col. Joe Mueller（美国海军陆战队退役人员）以"员工旅程"的概念为每一天制定了计划。吃完早餐，向美国国旗敬礼后，我们就出发了。准确地说，"像一群乌龟一样"。

我们通常会在岛上的一个高地开始新的一天——美国战争纪念馆（72号山丘）、埃德森岭或"Gifu"（27号山丘）。根据1942年海军陆战队第一师周边的一部分，我们进行了地图演习并规划了每日行动。

我们的旅行并非是一场以游客中心礼品店结束的大巴之旅。为了鸟瞰战场，我们徒步穿越了山脊和山谷小径，与挥舞着砍刀的当地人一起突破茂密的丛林。我们的目标始终是在地形上行走、在泥泞中跋涉、并从尽可能多的有利位置观察战场。

这次旅行超出了我的预期十倍。六个月后，我才刚刚开始回想我在瓜达尔卡纳尔岛所做和所见的事情。我与我的分队分享的经历、数十年的研究在我脑海中浮现的图像、以及这些图像所揭示的情感，实在是太震撼了，无法在这里全部讲述。我怀疑我需要用余生来充分表达这一切。

我有一个观察——我相信这一观察对于所有军事历史学家来说都是正确的，无论你的具体研究兴趣是什么。这个观察则是，你只有经历了才能真正了解！研究和地图研究并不能替代在战场上行走的经历。经过对瓜达尔卡纳尔岛战役的几十年研究，我以为我已经知道了一切。我以为我知道奥斯汀山的斜坡有多陡。我以为我知道伦加河有多宽。我以为萨沃岛远一些，图拉吉岛近一些。我以为我知道在锋利的白茅草中行走是什么感觉。我以为我知道炎热和潮湿是多么令人压抑。但是，我在这些方面的理解都是错的。再加上数月持续战斗带来的疲惫、口渴、饥饿、疾病、腐烂和蚊子——我的理解甚至不能与1942年南太平洋战争的现实相比较。哦，我有没有提到没有人试图杀了我们？

无论你的历史研究聚焦于何处，请到那里去经历！除非你经历过，否则你无法真正了解。

Jeff Ballard

加州亨廷顿比奇

2023年12月22日

The Roman Army of the Mid-Republic: From Conscription to Volunteer Service

Mary Jo Davies

American Military University

Abstract

The Roman army of the mid-Republic was known as the manipular legion, a unique tactical structure which remained in force for roughly 200 years (*c.* 315–107 BC). Up until the Second Punic War (218–201 BC), the Roman army had been a temporary militia based entirely on conscripted terms of service, which the Senate resupplied as needed. Property ownership was obligatory for recruitment. However, during the prolonged conflict of the Second Punic War, Rome had obtained a large overseas empire, which required permanent provincial garrisons. To recruit as many men as possible, the army occasionally suspended the property requirement for service in the legions. Attracted to the modest military pay and the prospect of a share of war booty a large number from the poorest social class began to volunteer for service in the legions. Over the ensuing decades, the Roman army began its gradual transition away from conscription and toward volunteer service. Polybius's detailed description of the mid-Republican army, combined with the nature of Rome's imperialistic endeavors, will be helpful in understanding the cause of this transition.

Keywords: maniple, hastati, principes, triarii, velites, cohorts, pilum, gladius hispaniensis

El ejército romano de la República Media: del servicio militar obligatorio al servicio voluntario

Resumen

El ejército romano de mediados de la República se conocía como la legión manipular, una estructura táctica única que permaneció en vigor durante aproximadamente 200 años (c. 315-107 a. C.). Hasta la Segunda Guerra Púnica (218-201 a. C.), el ejército romano había sido una milicia temporal basada completamente en condiciones de servicio reclutadas, que el Senado reabastecía según fuera nece-

doi: 10.18278/mhc.1.2.2

sario. La propiedad de la propiedad era obligatoria para la contratación. Sin embargo, durante el prolongado conflicto de la Segunda Guerra Púnica, Roma había obtenido un gran imperio de ultramar, que requería guarniciones provinciales permanentes. Para reclutar tantos hombres como fuera posible, el ejército suspendió ocasionalmente el requisito de propiedad para el servicio en las legiones. Atraídos por la modesta paga militar y la perspectiva de una parte del botín de guerra, un gran número de personas de la clase social más pobre comenzó a ofrecerse como voluntario para servir en las legiones. Durante las décadas siguientes, el ejército romano comenzó su transición gradual desde el servicio militar obligatorio hacia el servicio voluntario. La descripción detallada de Polibio del ejército republicano medio, combinada con la naturaleza de los esfuerzos imperialistas de Roma, será útil para comprender la causa de esta transición.

Palabras clave: manípulo, hastati, principes, triarii, velites, cohortes, pilum, gladius hispaniensis

罗马共和国中期的罗马军队：从征兵到志愿服务

摘要

罗马共和国中期的罗马军队被称为"中队制军团"，这是一种独特的战术结构，持续了大约200年（约公元前315年至公元前107年）。直到第二次布匿战争（公元前218年至公元前201年）之前，罗马军队一直是一支完全按照征兵服役的临时民兵，元老院根据需要进行补给。财产所有权对征兵而言是必需的。然而，在第二次布匿战争的长期冲突中，罗马获得了一个庞大的海外帝国，这需要长期的省级驻军。为了招募尽可能多的人，军队有时会暂停关于s军团服役的财产要求。微薄的军饷和战利品分享的可能性吸引了来自最贫困社会阶层的大量人群，他们开始自愿加入军团。在接下来的几十年里，罗马军队开始逐渐从征兵制过渡到志愿服务。波利比乌斯对罗马共和国中期军队的详细描述，结合罗马帝国主义事业的性质，将有助于理解这一转变的原因。

关键词：中队，青年兵，壮年兵，后备兵，少年兵，步兵队，罗马重标枪，西班牙短剑(gladius hispaniensis)

The city of Rome came together as a monarchy on the banks of the Tiber River on the western coast of central Italy around 753 BC. Over the course of nearly two-hundred and fifty years, its rulers became increasingly corrupt forcing the city to make a radical decision. In 509 BC, Rome abolished the monarchy and established a Republic with a mixed constitution.[1] Though the city owed its prosperity to trade in its early years, warfare made it a formidable force in the ancient world. Yet Rome had always been too busy conquering the Italic peninsula to chronicle the story of their origins. The regal period and the early republic are, in fact, the most poorly documented periods of Roman history; it would take another five-hundred years for historians to consider recording the story of their roots. Such writers include, among others: first century Roman historian Titus Livius (Livy) (59 BC–17 AD) in *The History of Rome,* as well as Greek historian Dionysius of Halicarnassus (60-7 BC) in *The Roman Antiquities.* Dionysius stated that previous writers of Roman history, such as second century BC Greco-Roman historian Polybius (*c.* 200–*c.* 118 BC), "touched only in a summary way upon the early events that followed the founding of the city."[2] However, by the first century BC, archeological and epigraphic sources were not enough to create a comprehensive narrative of their past. Rome's origins, Livy states, traced "back beyond 700 years."[3] Time had claimed much of it, leaving behind many historical gaps. To fill the voids they crafted legends—such as that of Romulus and Remus—which made it

exceedingly difficult to separate fact from folklore.

Historical literature written in the first century BC extended well beyond Rome's origin story, but the narratives were still oddly deficient, albeit in different ways and for different reasons. While the common themes concerned politics and war through the centuries, historians of this period did not incorporate details regarding the composition of the Roman military. Historian Adrian Goldsworthy suggests that this might be because such details would have already been well-known and thus, redundant.[4] Clearly, he was referring to Polybius. While Polybius' influential narrative in the *Histories* did not incorporate Rome's origin story, it did offer the most comprehensive, detailed data regarding the organization, tactics, and equipment of the Roman army during the period of the mid-Republic (264–133 BC). By this time Rome had already conquered most of the Italian Peninsula, hence Polybius's focus was primarily on the efforts it took for ancient Rome to extend its imperial power beyond Italy, particularly when it came to Carthage.

There were three wars that Rome waged against Carthage, one of the most affluent cities of the classical world located on the northern coast of Africa. These are known as the Punic Wars, the first of which Rome waged to gain influence over the strategic city of Messana on the island of Sicily.[5] The accounts regarding the First and Second Punic Wars (264–241 BC and 218–201 BC) depended on stories orally handed down since Polybius was born after these battles took place. He was, however, eyewitness to the Third Punic War (149–146 BC) making the final bloody conflict quite easy for him to write about.

In the *Histories* Polybius explains that the Roman army of the mid-Republic was known as the manipular legion. Its structure—explained in further detail below—remained in force for roughly 200 years (*c.* 315–107 BC).[6] Up until the Second Punic War, the Roman army had been a temporary militia based entirely on conscripted terms of service, which the Senate resupplied as needed. Property ownership was obligatory for recruitment.[7] The prolonged conflicts of the Second Punic War were often disastrous, but they had galvanized Roman resistance. By implementing skillful defensive strategies, Rome ultimately secured hegemony over the western Mediterranean despite its many misfortunes on the battlefield. This expansion required permanent

Figure 1. The stele of Kleitor depicting Polybius, Hellenistic art, 2nd century BC, Museum of Roman Civilization. Licensing: this media file is in the public domain.

provincial garrisons and necessitated an increasing number of recruits to replace the devastating legionary losses. In an effort to make up for a growing deficit of propertied men, Rome occasionally suspended the land requirement for service. Attracted by the modest military pay, a large number of volunteers from the poorest social class began to join the legions. Over the ensuing decades, the Roman army began its gradual transition away from conscription and toward volunteer service. A concise sketch of Polybius's description of the mid-Republican army, combined with the nature of Rome's imperialistic endeavors, will be helpful in understanding the cause of this transition.

The organization of Rome's *early* military is a subject for which the surviving evidence is too limited to provide a detailed description. A major development did occur during the mid-regal period in the sixth century BC when Rome adopted the hoplite system of warfare. Hoplite warfare had developed in the early seventh century BC in Greece and spread from there to the Greek colonies in southern Italy.[8] The Romans conventionally attributed the adoption of the hoplite phalanx to King Servius Tullius who reigned between 578 and 534 BC. It was not until the second century BC when Polybius offered a thorough, carefully researched description of the Roman military as it existed between 264 and 146 BC.

The Roman legion of the mid-Republic comprised three rows, each containing ten tactical units called maniples. Commanded by two centuri-ons and two rear-guard assistants called *optiones,* each maniple in the first two rows contained two centuries of sixty men for a total of one-hundred twenty men per maniple. The ten maniples in the third row each had one century of sixty men. [9] The total number of men per legion amounted to three-thousand. The gaps between the maniples in each row were equal in width to the frontage of a maniple, which, in turn, was the equivalent of twenty forward-facing men spaced roughly two feet apart from each other. To cover the gaps between the maniples, the military staggered each row.

The Roman army at this time was extremely hierarchical; its structure was organized on wealth, age, and social standing. Organized in a battle line three rows deep called the *triplex acies,* the legion's youngest and least skilled men—typically soldiers in their teens and early twenties called *hastati*—occupied the first row of the legion. The second row comprised men in the prime of life—usually in their mid-twenties and thirties—called the *principes.* The men in the third row, known as the *triarii,* were the oldest and most experienced soldiers.[10] Recruited from the youngest, poorest civilians, roughly twelve-hundred light infantry skirmishers known as *velites* stood in front of each legion (see Figure 2). By disrupting and confusing the enemy line, the *velites* made it easier for the higher-ranking soldiers to then step in for combat. However, being the first to confront the enemy made them a sacrificial component of the Roman army. Many lost their lives even before the battle was in full swing.

THE MANIPULAR LEGION

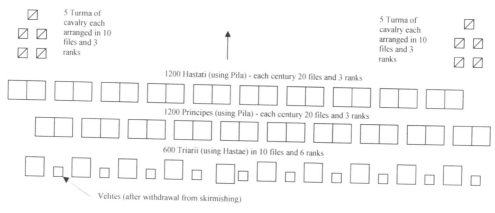

5 Turma of cavalry each arranged in 10 files and 3 ranks

5 Turma of cavalry each arranged in 10 files and 3 ranks

1200 Hastati (using Pila) - each century 20 files and 3 ranks

1200 Principes (using Pila) - each century 20 files and 3 ranks

600 Triarii (using Hastae) in 10 files and 6 ranks

Velites (after withdrawal from skirmishing)

Figure 2. Roman manipular disposition after deployment, but before engagement. Licensing: this media file is in the public domain.

Adjoining the manipular legion were the *alae* (wings) who were not Roman, but recruited from the allied cities of Italy. The typical size of an *ala* depended on the campaign. Polybius states, "the Consuls send orders to the magistrates of the allied cities in Italy, from which they determine that allied troops are to serve: declaring the number required, and the day and place at which the men selected must appear."[11] Flanking the *alae* were the cavalrymen known as the *equites*—young aristocrats from the wealthiest Roman class with a titled privilege that allowed them to have their horses refunded when killed in battle.[12] There were three-hundred cavalrymen per legion, which the military divided into ten squadrons—thirty men each—called *turmae*. Three *decurions* commanded each squadron with the assistance of three *optiones*. Ten campaigns of military service were mandatory for the cavalrymen to be able to subsequently serve in public office.[13]

Wealth also played a significant role in the distribution of weapons in the mid-Republican army. Each *velite* carried several thinly constructed javelins. While being the first to confront the enemy put them at a serious disadvantage, Polybius states that the officers had to observe whether the *velites* showed "courage or the reverse on confronting dangers."[14] However, their pay was not dependent on their performance, nor did they benefit from a share of war booty.[15] In contrast, the legionary soldiers benefitted from significant protection. The *hastati* carried two different types of large javelins, one heavier than the other. Known as the *pilum*, this weapon had tremendous plunging power (see Figure 4). The *triarii* and *principes* carried a longer spear known as the *hastae*. All soldiers carried a sidearm—a short dagger called the *pugio*. Around the early second century BC, the Romans replaced the *pugio* with a larger version known as the *gladius hispaniensis*—the Spanish short sword (see Figure 3). The cavalryman each carried a sturdy lance and shield, which, as Polybius states, they copied from the Greeks.[16] Their spear came with a butt spike which they could use as a secondary weapon. They, too, carried a *gladius*, although it was likely larger than that used by the infantry and which they employed when they lost or destroyed their spears.[17]

Wealthy soldiers wore a mail armor made of metal called the *loricae* (see Figure 5) and carried a rectangular convex shield called a *scutum,* which was two feet in width and four feet in length. In contrast, the *velites* wore a small square brass plate over their chest and carried a sturdy shield, round in shape called a *parma,* which had a diameter of about three feet.[18] All warriors wore metal helmets, but the *velites'* headgear was crestless. Sometimes they wrapped their helmet with wolf fur so that the officers could recognize them as *velites.* All other soldiers had three feathers in either the color purple or black arranged on the crest of their helmets.[19]

When it came to fighting strategies in the Republican army, the tactical space each soldier needed on the battlefield was considerably greater than that of the Greek or Macedonian hoplites, since Romans did not fight as a tightly-packed collective military unit. While each Roman soldier was part of a group called the maniple, they fought individually. Polybius states:

Figure 3. The gladius hispaniensis—or Spanish short sword—which originated in Iberia. This double-edged blade became the standard sword of the Roman army from the second century BC, after the Punic Wars. Licensed under the Creative Commons.

[A]s their method of fighting admits of individual motion for each man—because he defends his body with a shield, which he moves about to any point from which a blow is coming, and because he uses his sword both for cutting and stabbing,—it is evident that each man must have a clear space, and an interval of at least three feet both on flank and rear, if he is to do his duty with any effect.[20]

Polybius seems to suggest that the soldiers' flanks included three feet of space on either side, which presumably left three feet of corporal space that the soldier himself *and* his equipment occupied, for a total tactical clearance of about nine feet per soldier in each maniple. But, according to historian Michael J. Taylor, such a line-up would have taken up too much field space. A more reasonable setup submits that the three feet of space on the soldiers flanks included the physical space that the soldier himself occupied, thus leaving just under two feet of open space on either side of each soldier. This meant that each soldier controlled six feet of tactical clearance rather than nine.[21] Either way, this manipular arrangement implies that the Roman soldiers fought in a more open-order formation than the densely packed Greek-style phalanx.

Some scholars have doubted—even criticized—Polybius's claim that Roman soldiers always operated in such an open-order formation. Their criticism relies on information provided by fourth century AD Roman writer Flavius Vege-

tius Renatus (Vegetius), who claimed that when necessary (especially when the battlefield was small) Roman soldiers did fight in tight formation similar to that of the Greek phalanx.[22] In Book III of *De Re Militari*, Vegetius states that if the battlefield was not spacious enough, it would be "more advantageous to engage in close order than to extend your line too much."[23] However, it is important to keep in mind that unlike Polybius, Vegetius was far-removed from the period of history he was covering, having been born roughly six hundred years after the Punic Wars took place. More significantly, the fighting tactics as suggested by Vegetius would have presented serious strategic problems for the Roman infantry of the mid-Republic. Their army included launching weapons, such as the *pila,* as well as slashing/thrusting weapons like the *gladii.* These necessitated ample elbow room since operating them required their arms to swing about in various directions. In fact, Taylor states that the Roman soldier required significant space if only to prevent him from accidentally slicing his brother warriors.[24] Greek phalanxes, on the other hand, used only one type of weapon: a forward thrusting spear, which is what allowed them to fight in tightly packed formation.

To the extent that the enemy did not overpower them, the Roman army preserved their spacing while fighting. They also maintained the inter-manipular gaps throughout the duration of the conflict. Nevertheless, these gaps allowed for a very flexible, accordion-style legion which made it possible for the commanders and subordinates

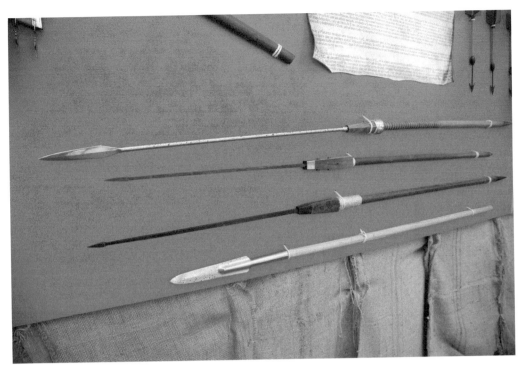

Figure 4: Various pila of the Roman Republic—heavy Roman spears, approximately seven feet in length. The shaft was made of wood and was about four feet in length; the tip was made of iron and was about three feet in length. Licensed under the Creative Commons.

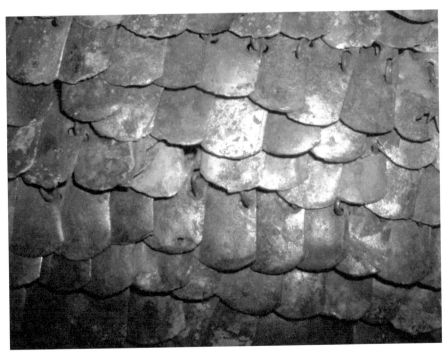

Figure 5: Detail of a Roman scale armour called the loricae. Each plate has six holes. The scales are then linked together in rows. Licensed under the Creative Commons.

to easily expand or—to a limited extent—shrink their line of defense based on the nature of the terrain, the character of the troops, or the strength and disposition of the enemy. The gaps also discouraged the enemy soldiers from penetrating, since Roman missile crossfire often overwhelmed these empty spaces. This kind of military elasticity, if properly maintained, ultimately helped the Romans to preserve the tactical integrity of the entire legion. They prevented panicky, less experienced soldiers from becoming intermingled with other units. Without these gaps the Roman maniples risked becoming a muddled, confused mass. Indeed, they risked defeat if they became too compact, such as happened at the Battle of Cannae in 216 BC, where Polybius reported that the Carthaginians pressed the Romans together and annihilated them.[25] Fifty-seven thousand Roman infantry faced roughly twenty-five thousand men at the center of the Carthaginian line, which was composed of Celt and Spaniard Carthaginian allies. The weight of the much larger Roman center pushed the smaller Carthaginian center back, eventually creating a concave enemy line in which the Romans soon found themselves trapped. The African flank units of the Carthaginian army then enveloped the Roman legions, compressing them into a disorganized body. Losing their manipular spacing, the Romans were unable to use their weapons effectively, causing the Carthaginians to slaughter them *en masse*.[26] As Polybius stated, "the circle becoming more and more contracted, they at last were all killed on the field."[27]

Since property ownership was a requirement for service, the census kept a record of land-owners from which the Senate selected men for mandatory conscription once a year, every year. What Rome did not have was a permanent standing army of professional soldiers. Polybius states that after the draft,

> the military tribunes dismiss them to their homes. But when the day has arrived on which they were all bound by their oath to appear at the place named by the Consuls (for each Consul generally appoints a separate place for his own legions, each having assigned to him two legions and a moiety of the allies), all whose names were placed on the roll appear without fail.[28]

Furthermore, throughout the mid-Republic, the army remained a temporary militia, which disbanded at the end of each battle. As for terms of service, Polybius states that all those selected for the legions must serve twenty years before they reach the age of forty-six, although the army did not require any man to serve in more than sixteen campaigns.[29]

Each battle took the life of thousands of men, but without a standing army of skilled soldiers, Rome had to constantly secure speedy training of new recruits. Perhaps Rome's unmitigated, humiliating disaster at Cannae, was due, in part, to the hasty training of rookies. Compounding this problem were the difficulties faced by the cavalry. Apart from the fact that Rome likely recruited inexperienced *equites* as young as seventeen years of age, all ancient cavalrymen lacked stirrups. The rider could not generate the necessary leverage to pull the lance out of his victim without running the risk falling off his horse.[30]

Over time, the transient nature of the Roman system developed a string of serious disadvantages—exacerbated by Rome's expansion outside of the Italian peninsula. Land-owning farmers formed the majority of the recruits. Away from home for long stretches at a time caused an inordinate amount of hardship and sometimes financial ruin for their families since there was often no one to help till the soil or provide support for the harvests. A man's lengthy absence from home also made child-bearing—the future land-owning soldiers of Rome—more difficult. Furthermore, the acquisition of overseas provinces required large permanent provincial garrisons, which forced soldiers to spend even longer periods away from home in continuous military service. Service in the legions had become an unenthusiastic drudgery—not something Rome could afford if they wanted to hold on to hegemonic power.

For much of its existence, the army of the mid-Republic was always at war. Whether they were defensive campaigns; whether they reflected a desire for economic gain, or whether their initial goal had always been universal supremacy, scholars have been debating these issues since ancient times and continue to debate them in the modern age. Some ancient historians had a more favorable opinion of the wars of the mid-Republic than others. When comparing the tumultuous conflicts of the late Republic to those of the mid-Republic, Roman statesman Marcus Tullius Cicero (108–43 BC) criticized the ever-growing lust for personal ambition of certain politicians of the first century BC. He stated that while their forefathers ruthlessly annihilated Carthage during the Punic Wars they had "some special reason for what they did."[31] That reason, Cicero stated, was because the "Carthaginians violated treaties."[32] Contrarily, the men of the late Republic began to use the army as an instrument in service of their own personal ambitions.[33]

Polybius's assessment of the mid-Republican wars was not as favorable as Cicero's. He highlighted Rome's ruthless aim for universal power especially after the success of the First Punic War. Though he believed that Roman success in the Punic wars was the result of discipline, "[i]t was not," he recognized, "by mere chance or without knowing what they were doing that the Romans struck their bold stroke for universal supremacy and dominion, and justified their boldness by its success."[34]

Whatever their motives, scholarship knows for certain that the result of the mid-Republican wars was the acquisition of land, which directly benefited the Roman people. Success and prosperity, however, became a bench test for the survival of the Republic. The impulse to exploit their authority became ever stronger when executed from a position of growing supremacy.[35] After the Third Punic War, demographic and territorial expansion did not witness a corresponding rise in land available for cultivation by country dwellers. Much of the land acquired during this period came increasingly under the control of aristocrats. The inevitable outcome was a rise in rural poverty, which created a growing male citizen population unable to meet the property requirement for military service.[36]

After the catastrophic losses of the Second Punic War, the lack of landed servicemen forced the Senate to occasionally drop the property requirement for service. In times of emergency, they recruited legionary soldiers from the poorest citizen-class: the so-called proletarians. These were men who did not own property. But despite the problems the military was facing with the propertied class, Rome was reluctant to completely abandon the militia system of conscripted, propertied servicemen.[37] It would take consul Gaius Marius's (157–86 BC) need to strengthen his forces for the Jugurthine War (112 BC–106 BC) to catalyze new changes to the Roman army. A consistent shortage of landed servicemen compelled Marius to break from tradition, which, as stated, typically turned to proletarian recruitment only in time of emergency. Marius recruited soldiers from the poorest social class, but his need was not so much emergency as it was to secure a quick victory and a triumph back home. This action, in 107 BC, would begin to alter the overall composition of the Republican army, which eventually abolished the hierarchical structure based on wealth, age, and social standing by phasing out the

divisions of *hastati, principes, triarii* and *velites*. All soldiers became equal, highly trained heavy infantry, each carrying a *pilum* and a *gladius,* which the military now provided for them—since poor recruits still could not afford to buy their own weapons.[38] Known as the Marian reforms, this new system also replaced the three-lined manipular legion with a three-lined structure of ten cohorts. Furthermore, since the Social War (91–87 BC) granted citizenship to all peoples of the Italian peninsula, they also eliminated the *alae* division. Now all soldiers—allied and Roman—fought together in the legions. Over time, military service became a career that poor men pursued and which lasted for much of their adult life.

However, despite their eagerness to join the military, recompense was never sufficient enough, especially considering the growing political corruption and civil wars at home.[39] Driving many of these crises was a concern regarding the resettlement of returning soldiers. It became evident that more radical military reform was essential. Around the time of Caesar (100 BC–44 BC), the military pay increased twofold—from 112.5 *denarii* per year to 225. The slow but steady move away from propertied soldiers during the second century BC, led to an ever-increasing recruitment of the proletarian class, but, Rome still had not implemented a permanent standing army of professionally trained soldiers.[40]

In spite of the enduring success of their constitution, the Republic's system of checks and balances ultimately floundered. Continued conflicts drove them ever closer to a system of one-man rule.[41] In 30 BC, Roman statesman Octavian (63 BC–14 AD) defeated Roman politician Mark Antony (83 BC–30 BC) and his lover, the Egyptian queen Cleopatra (51 BC–30 BC) at the Battle at Actium (32 BC–30 BC). Octavian, as well as the majority of the Roman Senate, had seen Antony's romance with the Egyptian queen as a threat to the unity and hegemony of Rome. Cleopatra's ambition was to strengthen the Ptolemaic kingdom of Egypt. To this end, she used Antony's influence as well as that of her eldest son Caesarion—born from her previous relationship with Julius Caesar. Caesarion was a likely claimant to the throne of Egypt, but his ascension would have potentially handed Rome's hegemony over to Egypt and made Rome an Egyptian province. In August of 30 BC, Octavian ordered the death of seventeen-year-old Caesarion. This effectively converted Egypt into a Roman province.[42] Both Antony and Cleopatra died by their own hands soon afterward. On January 16, 27 BC, the Senate proclaimed Octavian Emperor of Rome by conferring the title of *augustus* on him. Thereafter, Octavian became known as Augustus, the first emperor of Rome. One of his earliest missions was to create a permanent standing army and he did so by definitively transforming the military from a combination of conscripts and volunteers to an all-volunteer standing army of long-term highly trained soldiers, regardless of financial or social standing.

About the Author

Mary Jo Davies is a graduate of history, having earned her Master's Degree in ancient and medieval studies from American Public University in 2018. She spends her time researching and writing articles for publication in scholarly journals. Although she writes on a variety of topics, her primary focus is on warfare in the ancient world. Apart from her journal contributions, she is compiling her published articles into a book encompassing warfare from the late Bronze Age through the end of the Roman Republic.

Bibliography

Primary Sources

Cicero, Marcus Tullius. *De Officis*. The Perseus Catalog. Accessed December 16, 2022. http://www.perseus.tufts.edu/hopper/

Dionysius of Halicarnassus. *The Roman Antiquities*. Translation by Earnest Cary, Ph.D. Cambridge: Harvard University Press, 1937. Archive.org. Accessed December 1, 2022. https://archive.org/details/romanantiquities01dionuoft/page/20/mode/2up?view=theater.

Polybius. *Histories*. The Perseus Catalog. Accessed December 8, 2022. http://www. perseus.tufts.edu/hopper/

Titus Livius (Livy). *The History of Rome*. The Perseus Catalog. Accessed December 1, 2022. http://www.perseus.tufts.edu/hopper/

Vegetius. *De Re Militari*. Translation by Dr. James Harper and Professor Lucille Adet (Dubai: Harper McLaughlin Adet Publications, 2019).

Secondary Sources

Boatwright, Mary T. et al. *The Romans: from Village to Empire*. 2nd Edition. New York: Oxford University Press, 2012.

Champion, Craige B. "Polybius on Political Constitutions, Interstate Relations, and Imperial Expansion." *Academia.edu*. Accessed December 16, 2022. http://www.academia.edu.

Cary, M. and H. H. Scullard. *A History of Rome*. 3rd Edition. Hampshire: Palgrave, 1975.

Daly, Gregory. *Cannae: The Experience of Battle in the Second Punic War*. London: Routledge Taylor & Francis Group, 2002.

Davies, Mary Jo. "Polybius on the Roman Republic: Foretelling a Fall." *Saber and Scroll* 4 no. 2 (2015): 93-106.

De Ligt, Luuk. "Roman Manpower Resources and the Proletarianization of the Roman Army in the Second Century BC." In *The Impact of the Roman Army (200 B.C. – A.D. 476): Economic, Social, Political, Religious and Cultural Aspects*. Edited by Lukas de Blois and Elio Lo Cascio. Boston: Brill, 2007.

Goldsworthy, Adrian. *The Complete Roman Army*. London: Thames & Hudson, 2011.

_____. *Roman Warfare*. Reprint edition. New York: Basic Books, 2019.

Harris, William V. *War and Imperialism in Republican Rome: 327–70 BC*. New York: Oxford University Press, 1979.

Le Glay, Marcel, et al. *A History of Rome*. 4th ed. Malden: Wiley-Blackwell Publishing Company, 2009.

Lendon, J. E. "War and Society." In *The Cambridge History of Greek and Roman Warfare*, Vol. 1. Edited by Phillip Sabin, Hans Wees, and Michael Whitby. Cambridge: Cambridge University Press, 2007.

Samuels, Martin. "The Reality of Cannae." *Militärgeschichtliche Mitteilungen Zeitschrift* 47, 1 (1990), 7-32.

Taylor, Michael J. "Visual Evidence for Roman Infantry Tactics." *Memoirs of the American Academy in Rome* 59/60 (2014/2015): 103-120.

Watson, G. R. "The Pay of the Roman Army. The Republic." *Zeitschrift für Alte Geschichte* 7 no. 1 (1958), 113-120.

Endnotes

1   Rome understood that monarchies, aristocracies, and democracies—on their own—tended to deviate into their evil twins: tyranny, oligarchy, and ochlocracy. To counteract this and avoid collapse, Rome combined all three elements into one governing body and included a system of checks and balances that would help each group to develop a respectful relationship with the other. The highest-ranking officials were the consuls who represented the monarchic element; the senate (made up of noblemen) represented the aristocratic element; and the Roman citizens made up the democratic element.

2   Dionysius of Halicarnassus, *The Roman Antiquities,* 1.6.2, trans. Earnest Cary, Ph.D. Cambridge: Harvard University Press, 1937. Archive.org. Accessed December 1, 2022. https://archive.org/details/romanantiquities01dionuoft/page/20/mode/2up?view=theater; Note: the Roman province of the Greek city of Halicanarssus was located in Anatolia, present-day Turkey. The Greeks greatly influenced Roman culture. They had been colonizing the Italian peninsula since the eighth century BC. It was the Greeks—master writers for centuries—who taught the Romans the art of writing history.

3   Titus Livius (Livy), *The History of Rome* pr.4, The Perseus Catalog, accessed July 10, 2015, http://www.perseus.tufts.edu.

4   Goldsworthy, *The Complete Roman Army*, 27.

5   William V. Harris, *War and Imperialism in Republican Rome: 327–70 BC* (New York: Oxford University Press, 1979), 63; Mary T. Boatwright et al., *The Romans: from Village to Empire,* 2nd edition (New York: Oxford University Press, 2012), 95.

6   The manipular legion is also known as the Polybian legion, since it was on account of the historian's writings that scholarship came to know the composition of the Roman forces of the mid-Republic.

7   Goldsworthy, *The Complete Roman Army,* 26.

8   Adrian Goldsworthy, *Roman Warfare,* reprint edition (New York, Basic Books, 2019), 9.

9   Polybius, *Histories* 6.24, The Perseus Catalog, accessed December 16, 2022, http://www.perseus.tufts.edu; Marcel Le Glay, et al., *A History of Rome,* 4th ed. (Malden: Blackwell, 2009): 65. Despite the apparent association with the number "one-hundred," a century—in the ancient Roman military—may have never intended to refer to a count of "one-hundred." When concerning the maniples of the mid-republic, one century referred to sixty soldiers.

10   Polybius, *Histories,* 6.21.

11   Ibid., 6.21.

12   Goldsworthy, *The Complete Roman Army,* 27.

13   Gregory Daly, *Cannae: The Experience of Battle in the Second Punic War* (London: Routledge Taylor & Francis Group, 2002): 73.

14   Polybius, *Histories,* 6.22.

15   Martin Samuels, "The Reality of Cannae," *Militärgeschichtliche Mitteilungen Zeitschrift* 47, 1 (1990), 12-13.

16   Polybius, *Histories,* 6.25.

17   Gregory Daly, *Cannae,* 75.

18   Polybius, *Histories,* 6.22-23.

19   Ibid., 6.23.

20   Ibid., 18.30.

21   Michael J. Taylor, "Visual Evidence for Roman Infantry Tactics," *Memoirs of the American Academy in Rome* 59/60 (2014/2015): 105-106.

22   The exact birth and death years of Vegetius are not known.

23   Vegetius, "Book III Dispositions for Action: Proper Distances and Intervals," in *De Re Militari,* translation Dr. James Harper and Professor Lucille Adet (Dubai: Harper McLaughlin Adet Publications, 2019).

24   Taylor, "Visual Evidence for Roman Infantry Tactics," 106.

25   Polybius, *Histories,* 3.116.

26   Martin Samuels, "The Reality of Cannae," 24-25.

27   Polybius, *Histories,* 3.116.

28 Polybius, *Histories*, 6.26.

29 Ibid., 6.19; Goldsworthy, *The Complete Roman Army*, 26.

30 Gregory Daly, *Cannae*, 75.

31 Cicero, *De Officis* 1.35, *The Perseus Catalog*, accessed December 16, 2022, http://www. perseus.tufts.edu.

32 Ibid., 1.38.

33 Le Glay, et al., *A History of Rome,* 123.

34 Polybius, *Histories*, 1.63.

35 Craige B. Champion, "Polybius on Political Constitutions, Interstate Relations, and Imperial Expansion," Academia.edu, accessed April 1, 2014: 12. http://www.acade mia.edu.

36 Luuk De Ligt, "Roman Manpower Resources and the Proletarianization of the Roman Army in the Second Century BC," in *The Impact of the Roman Army (200 B.C. – A.D. 476): Economic, Social, Political, Religious and Cultural Aspects,* Eds. Lukas de Blois, Elio Lo Cascio (Boston: Brill, 2007), 20.

37 Goldsworthy, *The Complete Roman Army*, 49.

38 M. Cary and H. H. Scullard, *A History of Rome,* 3rd ed. (New York: Palgrave, 1975): 219; Goldsworthy, *The Complete Roman Army*, 44-47.

39 The civil wars were conflicts that plagued the last century of the Roman Republic between 88 BC and 28 BC, and led to the inevitable transition to Principate and the undisputed authority of one man.

40 G. R. Watson, "The Pay of the Roman Army. The Republic." *Zeitschrift für Alte Geschichte* 7 no. 1 (1958): 119-120.

41 Mary Jo Davies, "Polybius on the Roman Republic: Foretelling a Fall," *Saber and Scroll* 4 no. 2 (2015): 101.

42 M. Cary and H. H. Scullard, *A History of Rome,* 297-298.

"Sew for Victory!" How Women During World War II Used Their Domesticity to Aid the Cause

Aisha Manus

Independent Historian

Abstract

At the beginning of WWII, roughly 50 percent of American women knew how to sew. By 1944, that number jumped to 82 percent. This jump was in large part due to a major push by the government and the media for American women to support the efforts on the Homefront through the domesticity already expected of them. From articles in women's magazines to posters released by the U.S. Government, women were told to "Sew for Victory." Supported, in large part by the American Red Cross allocated millions in funds, these women, in turn, produced tens of millions of bandages, quilts, and articles of clothing for the service members both at home and abroad, demonstrating that the domestic work of women is an essential part in the success of the war.

Keywords: Homefront, WWII, Sewing, Knitting, Quilting, Volunteerism, Red Cross, Women's History, Propaganda

"¡Coser para la victoria!" Cómo las mujeres durante la Segunda Guerra Mundial utilizaron su vida doméstica para ayudar a la causa

Resumen

Al comienzo de la Segunda Guerra Mundial, aproximadamente el 50 por ciento de las mujeres estadounidenses sabían coser. En 1944, esa cifra saltó al 82 por ciento. Este salto se debió en gran parte a un importante impulso por parte del gobierno y los medios de comunicación para que las mujeres estadounidenses apoyaran los esfuerzos en el frente interno a través de la domesticidad que ya se esperaba de ellas. Desde artículos en revistas femeninas hasta carteles publicados por el gobierno de Estados Unidos, a las mujeres se les decía "coser para la victoria". Con el apoyo, en gran parte, de fondos millonarios de la Cruz Roja Americana, estas mujeres, a su vez, produjeron decenas de millones de vendas, colchas y prendas

doi: 10.18278/mhc.1.2.3

de vestir para los miembros del servicio tanto en el país como en el extranjero, demostrando que el trabajo doméstico de Las mujeres son una parte esencial en el éxito de la guerra.

Palabras clave: Frente doméstico, Segunda Guerra Mundial, Costura, Tejido, Acolchado, Voluntariado, Cruz Roja, Historia de la Mujer, Propaganda

"为胜利而缝纫！"第二次世界大战期间妇女如何利用家庭生活来援助这一事业

摘要

二战初期，大约50%的美国妇女懂得缝纫。到1944年，这一数字跃升至82%。该数字跃升在很大程度上归因于政府和媒体大力推动美国妇女通过其已被期望的家庭生活来支持国土安全。从妇女杂志文章到美国政府发布的海报，妇女都被告知要"为胜利而缝纫"。在美国红十字会拨出数百万资金的支持下，美国妇女反过来为国内外的美国军人生产了数千万条绷带、被子和衣物，这表明妇女的家庭工作是战争成功的重要组成部分。

关键词：国土防线，二战，缝纫，针织、衲缝，志愿主义，红十字会，妇女历史，宣传

Pulitzer Prize winning historian Laurel Thatcher Ulrich once wrote, "Well-behaved women seldom make history."[1] While the phrase has gone on to inspire women everywhere to voice their opinions and smash the patriarchy, when I hear that phrase, I think of its original intention. All the untold stories of everyday women and the change they affected. When historians focus on the few who broke the mold, we are left with a history that is greatly lacking in the grand scheme of things. While those exceptional women are extremely important to history, the everyday heroes who made an impact by continuing to go about their lives are just as important. Their actions may have been small, but they created something great as a whole.

From the Revolutionary War until the present conflicts, American women have always been called upon to show their patriotism and support. From taking their husband's positions at work to free them for service, raising money to buy bonds, and even going to combat themselves, women have served their country in various ways. During World War II it was no different. Some women worked in bomb plants or other arms manufacturing or flew to distant places overseas to serve as nurses or members of the Women's Army Auxiliary Corp (WAAC) or United States Naval Reserves (Women's Reserve) (WAVES), but there were many who aided the cause from the Homefront, using the domestic skills they had honed for generations to make a difference without ever needing to step out of the gender roles they were expected to play at the time. Those are the women that this article will focus on in particular, on the work of women who sewed and knitted for the Red Cross between 1942 and 1945, with specific emphasis on items that were intended for the war front, rather than the Red Cross general fund.

At the start of the Revolutionary War, 1,644 women from across New England had already come together to engage in 46 spinning bees,[2] along with 192 women participating in the southern portion of the colonies,[3] to create homespun fabric and clothes as part of the economic protests that proceeded the war. When the Civil War broke out, women in both the Union and the Confederacy once again used their sewing skills to make quilts, uniforms, and kits to comfort soldiers fighting and to raise funds to support the troops. The United States Sanitary Commission even provided a pattern for the Union Soldiers' uniform.[4] This type of support and patriotism by women continued into the Spanish-American and First World Wars, and by the time the United States had entered into WWII,

American women had plenty of experience in using needlework for the cause. One woman, Mrs. Laura S. Litchfield of Milwaukee, WI, first began knitting for soldiers around the age of 13 during the Civil War and continued to do so with the Red Cross through the Spanish-American and First World War, knitting over 300 sweaters alone. In the first six months of 1942, at the age of 92, she had knitted another 71 sweaters and begun working on mufflers for the soldiers overseas.[5]

While most women were not as skilled as Mrs. Litchfield, that didn't stop women who wanted to serve from increasing their skills and trying. Prior to the war, 50 percent of American women knew how to sew. By 1944, that number jumped to 82 percent.[6] This uptick in skills was largely due to the classes that formed at sewing centers across the country, such as the class at the Pratt Institute in Brooklyn, where 400 women eagerly signed up for their class on reusing clothing remnants just three months after the attack on Pearl Harbor.[7] Because no new sewing machines were being made during the war, in an effort to free up factories for war goods,[8] to meet the demands of all the women looking to sew for the cause but who didn't have machines of their own, the Red Cross opened sewing rooms in office buildings, libraries, and churches across the country. The Red Cross also allocated funds to provide the fabric and materials to these rooms, with a budget of $2.1 million dollars in 1944 alone,[9] and they also established quotas and goals to motivate and inspire the women who joined.

Page 115 of the March 1944 issue of *McCall's* magazine. This advertisement for Singer sewing products was purposeful in its mention of their engagement in war work. During the war Singer stopped production of their sewing machines so that their factories could be used for the production of war-related items instead. The War Production Board made sure parts were still available to fix machines previously made so homemakers could continue sewing without disruption from the lack of new machines. (Photographed by Aisha Manus from her personal collection)

For example, in the Camden, South Carolina, Red Cross sewing room between September 1, 1942, and June 1, 1943, the Red Cross set a quota of 711 garments. With the 1,907 yards of material that the Red Cross headquarters sent them to accomplish this goal in that time frame, not only did they make that quota, but they also produced an additional 100 garments, plus used scraps left over to make patchwork quilts. On top of this, the women also made 150 kit-bags, also known as duffle bags, and 10 chair cushion covers for Fort Jackson and a Red Cross banner for Columbia Airbase. To achieve this, it took the work of "16 different groups of County Women sewing for us, 11 ladies in the Liberty Hill group, a group at Westville, groups at the two factories, 13 workers in the Boykin group, the Jewish Sisterhood and the Baptist Circle and a group in the Browning home," plus 27 individual sewers who lived in Camden.[10] Between January 1st and June 1st of 1944, the Camden chapter reported another 327 articles made, which they shipped to Fort Jackson, SC, for the Camp and Hospital Service Council.[11]

In Butts County, GA the women were sewing for the Red Cross even before the United States entered the war, with the items going to foreign relief. From January 1940 until May 1942, the women made 3619 articles, including 176 sweaters, 81 bedspreads, and 47 beanies, among other things.[12] From October 1942 until January 1943 they shipped out another 465 garments and four quilts. They also were finishing up four more quilts, all made from the scrap fabric from the garments.[13] In January of 1945, they had already sent 15 Navy sweaters, 21 Army sweaters, 101 stump socks, and 50 pairs of pajamas, and had cut 50 bed jackets and Army kits bags that just needed to be sewn, indicating another very productive year ahead of them.[14]

In nearby Jackson County, GA, in 1942, the Red Cross sewing rooms women sewed 2,199 garments and knitted 297 garments.[15] In the city of Jefferson, GA, the Red Cross sewing room, which was located in the City Hall, had to shut down production in late February 1942 because they had already run out of material and had to wait for a new shipment, according to the chapter director Mrs. H.I. Mobley.[16] However, three weeks later, they were back at it again, having already cut garments that needed sewing from 193 yards of recent-

ly arrived fabric.[17] The following year, the Jackson County chapter only sewed 670 garments; however, they increased their production of military-specific items such as Army mufflers, helmets, wristlets, and Navy sweaters, helmets, and caps.[18]

Not all chapters were as productive. In Houston County, GA, the chairman of the Red Cross workroom reported only 125 garments and 175 bags sewn by October 1942. She stated, "This work has been done under great difficulties as only a few women have done any of the sewing," even though 150 women had registered for sewing. She hoped that women would "take more interest in the sewing room."[19] In Athens, GA, the chairman of the Red Cross committee also found herself lacking women and stated that the "Red Cross desperately needs more volunteer workers among University students in summer school" and hoped that the new Red Cross volunteer course at the University of Georgia, Athens would bring them in. One of the topics to be taught was "sewing for service men [sic]," in addition to bandage rolling and first aid.[20]

To urge women to do their part by participating in a way that played for women's domesticity, President Roosevelt created the Office of War Information (OWI) on June 13, 1942, after enacting Executive Order 9182,[21] to provide not just war-related news to the general public but to also create the print advertisements and posters that would be used as propaganda.[22] In all, 56 posters were created that preached frugality and home efforts, or 16.6 percent of all posters created during the war.[23] One such poster, entitled "Sew For Victory," which played off these themes, was created by an artist by the name of Pistchal for the Federal Arts Project in New York in 1941, as part of the Works Project Administration (WPA).[24] The WPA was an organization that began in 1935 and provided employment to over 8.5 million Americans until it was disbanded in 1943, once the expansion of war industries provided full employment to the nation.[25] The Pitstchal poster depicted a sewing machine silhouette against a yellow and green background. Inside the silhouette was an image of a soldier at war surrounded by boats, tanks, and airplanes. The words "SEW FOR VICTORY" are above and below the silhouette.[26]

Another poster that was created that specifically targeted women who sew was a poster from 1943 entitled, "Use It Up – Wear It Out – Make It Do!" This poster further reinforced the gendered household roles by depicting a woman mending her husband's pants while he is wearing them as he sharpens his lawnmower blades, showing the division among labor between men and women.[27] Another poster, "Wanted for Victory," from 1942, depicted a family doing their part by recycling and urging them to either sell the scraps to a collector or give to a charity.[28] Though not directly related to sewing, posters like this did inspire W.B. Powell, the editor of the Jackson-Argus paper in Jackson, Georgia, to write an article about "pussyfooting around out-of-the-way places and peep[ing] into people's back

yards to see what iron and steel and rubber scrap is to be found" and how in his own yard he found "more than a thousand pounds, some 200 pounds of copper, brass and lead" and how he sold part of it to buy more notions for the local Red Cross sewing club.[29]

Since not everyone was using their scrap funds to buy notions for the Red Cross, in cooperation with the OPA, the Red Cross issued "Cinderella" stamps to promote their National "Sew and Save Week," which took place the last week of February. The stamps, which ran each year from 1939 to 1945, ranged in size from 2x1 inches to 3x2 inches and varied in colors as well as theme. Four of the seven stamps were patriotic in color, with the three from 1940, 1941, and 1942 advocating for participants to buy war bonds and to make 1 million home-sewn garments and the 1944 stamp having a soldier made of sewing notions. The other three used sewing notions in their images, with the 1939 stamp being blue, orange, and white, the 1943 stamp being green, white, and yellow, and the 1945 stamp being yellow and red.[30] Department stores, such as Belks in Clinton, South Carolina, hoping to capitalize off the fabric purchase for these Sew and Save weeks, would run ads in the local newspapers to remind customers of the dates and advertise the items they sold that supported this cause.[31] Other companies, such as Etheridge-Smith Company in Jackson, Georgia, ran generic "Sew and Save" ads during the week of the event that could still be used at a different point in the year.[32]

Sewing companies released booklets promoting frugality while promoting their products, such as the "Make and Mend" booklet from the Spool Cotton Company in 1942. To go along with these tactics, the Red Cross partnered with the Office of Price Administration and issued "Cinderella" stamps to promote their National "Sew and Save Week", which took place the last week of February. The stamps, which ran each year from 1939 to 1945, ranged in size from 2"x1" to 3"x2" and varied in colors as well as theme. Stores would often use that week to promote their supplies in hopes of capitalizing off this national promotion. (Photographed by Aisha Manus from her personal collection)

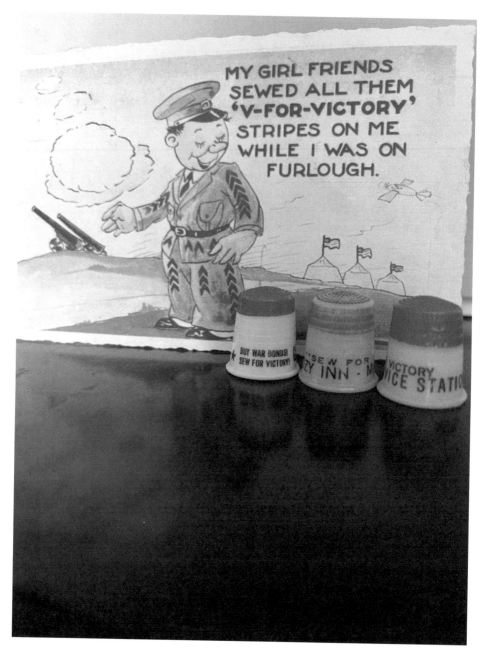

These three thimbles in the foreground were distributed by various businesses to show their support for the cause while simultaneously promoting themselves. The one on the left was from Gamler's Diamond Importers of Buffalo, NY. The middle thimble was from Cozy Inn in Martinton, IL. The thimble on the right is from Burke's Service Station, location unknown. The image in the background was a cheeky postcard sent from Craig Field, AL to Forest Hills, NY in December 1942. The message was two Cinderella stamps stuck to the back, one with "V for Victory" and the other "Speak up for Democracy".(Photographed by Aisha Manus from her personal collection)

Magazine and other media entities also perpetuated women's participation through domesticity, by forming the War Advertising Council, the Writers' War Board, and the Magazine Bureau of the Office of War Information and presenting their information through feature articles, short fiction, magazine advertisements, and columns.[33] This could be seen in an editorial in early 1943 in the *Evening Star*, out of Washington, D.C., which stated, "Sewing is a patriotic as well as practical pastime these days, and wise women everywhere are learning to fashion clothes for the family as well as to remodel and repair old garments."[34] Local papers also ran columns with these types of propaganda. In the March 12, 1942, issue of *The Forsyth County News* in Georgia, an article appeared that listed seven things farm women can "do as their part in Victory." The second item on the list called for the women to "do your own sewing. Make over [sic] old clothes and save all scraps as they may be used in bed quilts, quilted house coats [sic], pillows and draperies." They hoped this "patriotic yet practical appeal" would reach the "30-odd thousand FSA [Farm Service Agency] homemakers in the state."[35]

Even as the war was finally beginning to wind down, there was still a push to continue to conserve fabrics. In the 1945 book *Thread of Victory*, the author urged Americans to continue to make do with the clothing they had, saying,

The question then arises as to how much we can cut down. To help with the war, we can wear clothes that are patched and make it popular to do so. You ladies can wear a dress many times and be proud of its long wear and forget the question of new style. You can put aside the idea that one should not be seen twice in the same dress or in the same suit. We do not need a different outfit for every occasion nor a number of outfits hanging in the closet awaiting some future use. Must we buy new clothes just because spring or fall is here, or just because we are taking a trip? When we buy, we should think about how many clothes we have in the closet or even in the attic and what we can do with them. If we are not going to use them, they should be made available for those who will.[36]

In a 1942 booklet from Lilly Mills, a sewing thread company, Gertrude Duntz, the clothing supervisor of the Home Economics Division of the Pratt Institute, also addressed the concern some had about what they could do to help the cause. She wrote,

The old question of 'what can I do about it' must be solved for patriotism, as well as for budget comfort. This may seem irrelevant, but in the past the bees impressed our forefathers to such an extent that common tasks were so ved [sic] by sewing bees, and husking bees, and maybe you know of some other bees. Anyway, these gatherings, were high-tension parties where work was play. It is a good idea in this second horse and buggy age, to invite friends and have remodelling [sic] bees.[37]

Many women took this suggestion to heart, and sewing clubs and bees were formed all over the U.S. In Weston, MA, an affluent suburb of Boston, Louise Erickson, Beryl Fields, Frannie Thomas, and several other women started a group that continued to gather well into the 1990s. While it originally started as a mending and sewing group, according to Fields, it also served as a source of support for the women during a time when the men of the town were either working in the factories or serving overseas.[38]

There were also already established women's organizations that took up sewing during WWII to help the cause. The United Daughters of the Confederacy, who previously supported the Red Cross during WWI by forming units across the South and in doing so had made 3.5 million hospital garments and knitted another 100,000 regular garments,[39] once again had chapters working in the Red Cross Sewing rooms across the South to sew for the cause. In Clinton, South Carolina, in February 1943, the Stephen D. Lee chapter of the UDC sponsored work for the local Red Cross sewing room. One member, Mrs. Jessie Sparks, had already knitted ninety sweaters for "boys in the service in the past two years" even though her "health does not permit her to be active in many things ... seldom are her hands

idle."[40] Then, in April 1943, 18 members of the chapter met in the local Red Cross sewing room, which was located inside the city library, to fold surgical dressings,[41] an important job that the women did not take lightly. Volunteers for the Red Cross across the country are believed to have sewn and folded 2.5 billion surgical dressings.[42]

The American Legion Auxiliary also took advantage of Red Cross meeting rooms. In Clinton, South Carolina, they used the room to hold their meetings, where they would first hold a short business session and then finish their remaining time in the room doing Red Cross work. The president of this chapter, Mrs. B.O. Whitten, even made attendance mandatory.[43] Other groups, such as 4-H, also had members who participated in Red Cross sewing to further their leadership and volunteer skills. In Jefferson, Georgia, there were 34 girls from 4-H that sewed for the Red Cross in 1942,[44] and in neighboring Cumming, Georgia, there were 25 girls from 4-H that volunteered 400 hours to sew for the Red Cross that same year.[45] In Jackson, Georgia, there were several garden clubs that had Red Cross Sewing Subcommittees. There was the Jenkinsburg Garden Club, in which club president Mrs. Frank Childs, who also happened to be on the local Red Cross production Honor Roll that week,[46] stressed the importance of sewing and knitting for the organization.[47] There was also the Hawthorn Garden club, where, in the month of February 1943 alone, the members of the club sewed 100 garments.[48]

This poster, entitled "Sew For Victory", was created by an artist by the name of Pistchal for the Federal Arts Project in New York in 1941, as part of the Works Project Administration. The WPA, created in 1935, provided employment to over 8.5 million Americans until it was disbanded in 1943, when war industries provided full employment to the nation. (Photographed by Aisha Manus from her personal collection)

Since many of the countries that Hitler invaded were the previous homes of many recently immigrated Jews, the desire to help that cause was greatly magnified at times. While the Hadassah was the largest Jewish women's organization during the war, with a membership of nearly 120,000 women by the end,[49] it was the B'nai B'rith, a different Jewish service organization, that was actively doing their part to display their American patriotism by sewing for the Red Cross. At a meeting in October of 1944, the B'nai B'rith Women of Atlanta chapter president, Mrs. Sam A. Goldberg, called for more women to assist with the sewing group to speed up production, as it was imperative that B'nai B'rith women lend the Red Cross a hand as they were the organization doing the most for the man at the front as well as the for the civilian behind the line.[50] The call to action was clearly heard because by August of 1945, B'nai B'rith Women and Girls from across the country had made 5,000,000 surgical dressings and 400,000 sewn and knitted garments for the Red Cross.[51] This was up from the 3,750,000 total items they had sewn for the Red Cross by November of 1943.[52]

It was not just middle-class women that sewed for the Red Cross either. Former First Lady, Edith Wilson, who also sewed for the Red Cross during World War I, met every Wednesday with Mrs. Jesse Jones and Mrs. D. Buchanan Merriman at the Sulgrave Club to sew before lunch. Though she was very active herself, it was said that she stared "in amazement at the activity of the First Lady of World War II."[53] This was no surprise, considering that First Lady Eleanor Roosevelt carried the moniker "First Knitter of the Land" because she was often photographed carrying a large knitting bag that she took everywhere with her.[54]

Many women worked directly with the troops. At MacDill Field in Florida, the sewers for the Red Cross volunteered at the Post Enlisted Men's Service Club to patch, darn, or sew buttons on the soldiers' clothing there.[55] The soldiers stationed at Camp Gordon could have their buttons and insignia sewn on, and clothes mended at the Augusta, Georgia, USO club after the National Council of Catholic Women sponsored a Red Cross Sewing room there.[56] At the U.S. Army Air Corps barracks in Glendale, California, there was a "button brigade" made up of women who volunteered to sew on rank and mend ripped clothing.[57] In one instance, a woman indirectly boosted the morale of the soldiers with her sewing. Mrs. Archer of New Jersey sewed an apron for her daughter Jean, who was serving in the Red Cross overseas in Guam, and according to a letter from her daughter, "the sailors certainly get a kick out of my little red and white apron you made. 'Just like home,' they say."[58]

Not every woman or organization that was sewing for the troops was doing so through the Red Cross and its call for one million homespun garments. With the United Service Organizations operating approximately 3,000 USO clubs in the U.S., there were plenty of opportunities for women to sew for soldiers directly."[59] In Savannah, Georgia, the Hunter Army Airfield

On February 17, 1942, the War Production Board (WPB) enacted General Limitation Order L-85. Created to restrict the design of men's and women's fashion to save on domestic fabric production by up to 15 percent, gone were the ruffles, excessive pleats, and wide lapels, to be replaced by slim cuts and straight lines, as seen in Du Barry Perfect Pattern 5347 from 1942 or McCall Pattern 5913 from 1944. Some patterns even printed a "Bond of Guarantee" on their patterns to highlight that their patterns "conform exactly to the standard of measurements approved by the United States Department of Commerce," as seen on the back of Simplicity patterns of the era. (Photographed by Aisha Manus from her personal collection)

sewing committee of the USO-National Catholic Community Service Women's Division, also known as the Sew and Stitch Club,[60] spent every Friday from midday to as late as midnight sewing in the USO club. With more than 1000 hours of service for each member of the committee, from buttons to chevrons, they sewed so much that at one point, the base tailor complained that they were affecting his business![61]

This ability for women to tailor so well was an important skill during the course of the war because in 1942, after President Roosevelt created the War Production Board (WPB), he enacted Public Order 671. This order allowed for the production of things related to the armed forces to be prioritized over items of private interest. The WPB then enacted order L-85 on February 17, 1942, at a meeting attended by more than 800 fashion industry representatives, which restricted the design of men's and women's clothing to certain cuts and lengths, hoping to save 15 percent of domestic fabric production. Gone were ruffles, pleats, and wide lapels, to name a few things, and the hem of a woman's skirt had to be at least 17 inches from the ground.[62] The WPB hoped that these restrictions would prevent designers from creating new and different designs but instead keep the fashion styles similar to pre-war fashion so as not to influence women into buying the latest fashions and wasting precious resources, such as nylon, wool, or silk which were used for parachutes, uniforms, ammunition bags and other important textiles for war.[63] For every fifteen pairs of silk stockings not made, one powder bag could be made instead.[64] These silk powder bag were used in large caliber guns and because they burned away completely after use there was no need to clean the weapon between shots, saving precious time and effort on the battle field.[65]

Though the WPB restricted the use of wool from regular fashion, they still allowed women to receive wool through the Red Cross since they were knitting garments for soldiers.[66] Louise Stanely, chief of the Home Economics Bureau of the U.S. Department of Agriculture, even declared, "if the housewife doesn't know how to patch and darn, now is the time to learn."[67] The WPB also encouraged advertisers to post these restrictions, hoping to inspire patriotic women to save and sew accordingly.[68] The first women's magazine to do this was *Women's Wear Daily* in April 1942, followed by *Vogue* in May 1942.[69] In the June 1942 issue of *McCall's* magazine, they continued the trend, writing, "Right-about-face changes waste fabric, and the most patriotic thing we can do at present is to waste nothing. So your Government has asked designers not to waste materials on extreme changes, and to forego unnecessary flourishes on clothes, and to let the silhouette stay about where it is."[70]

On September 1, 1942, the WPB enacted Order L-153, which regulated home sewing patterns to fall under the guidelines of L-85.[71] On average, these new patterns would save about 1/8 yard per dress![72] However, some pattern companies were already producing patterns to meet the L-85 guidelines. In an advertisement in the *Jackson Herald* in Jefferson, Georgia, in June 1942, it was "patriotic to Sew and Save ... with the aid of our new Summer Book of Patterns. Just TEN CENTS for this bookful of smart, practical, fabric-saving designs for work, sports, and 'dress parade.'" Or you could send sixteen cents to the Newspaper Pattern Department and buy Pattern 9985, the Basque Frock, which required just 3.25 yards of 39-inch wide fabric for the size 16 and could be ordered in misses' and women's size 14, 16, 18, 20, 32, 34, 36, 38, 40, and 42.[73] The U.S. Treasury Department even encouraged women to buy patterns because "girls who make their own clothes bring us nearer to victory by putting their sewing savings into War Bonds."[74]

Taking it a step further, women were also encouraged to use the old men's suits, since they did not take their "civies" to war with them to create these new clothing designs.[75] In a 1942 sewing booklet from the Spool Cotton Company, hoping to financially benefit from the tie between winning the war and sewing at home, they showed women how to layout Vogue Patterns 9137 and 9001, a jacket and skirt, respectively, in a way that allows you to use the suit fabric effectively.[76] By reusing these fabrics, not only could one look "pretty and patriotic," but when they take "those old knockabouts and turn them into knockouts, [you] keep that glint in Uncle Sam's eye and still do your stint towards Victory!"[77] An article in *Ladies' Home Journal* in 1942 advised women to use their imagination to stretch their pennies by dyeing old coats, adding ribbon to the front of their dresses, or adding flaps to their pockets in the spirit of making do with what they already owned.[78] This sentiment was further emphasized in a 1944 article in *McCall's*, saying, "Yes, there are dozens of ways to turn a tired suit into a Cinderella garment. And you'll feel a warm glow of satisfaction knowing that you've followed the patriotic dictum to 'make do, make it over, make it last.'"[79]

By following this advice and remaking old clothes, women were honoring the Office of Price Administration's three-point "victory pledge," in which they asked housewives to "make and mend" by buying carefully, wasting nothing, and taking good care of everything.[80] One woman recalled that when her nylons lost their color, she would dip them into tea water to dye them naturally back[81] since many dyes were also restricted at this time due to the needs for chemicals in them for the war effort.[82] No longer was it shameful to wear mended clothing like in the era of the Great Depression, but rather, "A Patch is a Badge of Honor," according to government propaganda of the day.[83]

In some cases, women were actually rewarded for their ability to be thrifty. In November 1943, seventeen-year-old 4-H member Sue Batcheldor of Columbus, Georgia, was one of six Georgia state 4-H club winners, recognized for her "superior record in the current National 4-H Clothing Achievement activity" for her part in making and mending "183 of her own and family's old garments to help save vitally needed new cloth and labor for military uses." Her prize was a trip to Chicago for the National 4-H Club Congress, which was paid for by the Educational Bureau of the Spool Cotton Co.[84] The *Oregonian's* "Daily Home Magazine" also held a sewing contest for college girls during the war that gave out six 100-dollar war bonds to the winners,[85] while Harding College in Arkansas held a sewing contest for students during Sew and Save week, in which the first prize received material for a dress, while second and third prize was material for a blouse.[86]

Though most women did not receive much acknowledgment for their work, outside of a small blurb in the local newspapers' homemaker section, they occasionally received letters of thanks and gratitude. In February 1943, the women who sewed for the Red Cross sewing room in Clinton, South Carolina, received a letter from Pvt. Henry Young, Jr., who was serving in Africa, to thank them for a sweater and barracks bag they had made for him. They also received a letter from a Lt. Hugh Jacobs, stationed in Ireland, who was also very appreciative of a sweater he received.[87] The women of Camden, South Carolina, received a letter in June of 1943 from a Capt. S.E. Maislen, who was originally from Camden but was serving in Africa. In his letter, he wrote, "I always wondered where all those things the Red Cross women sewed went. Now I know. We have quite a batch of pajamas that our patients wear, which were made by the Red Cross."[88]

Junior enlisted and officers were not the only ones writing letters of thanks to the women for their efforts. In April 1945, the Commanding Officer of Hunter Army Airfield, Brigadier-General J. M. Fitzmaurice, wrote a letter to the sewing committee of the Nation Catholic Community Service, Women's Division, in Savannah, Georgia. In his letter he wrote,

> On behalf of the servicemen of Hunter Field, I wish to take this opportunity to express my sincere appreciation to you and your organization for the fine services you have rendered. It is my personal belief that you have aided materially in maintaining a high level of morale, which is a most important contribution to the mission of the Army Air Forces. It is very gratifying to me and I am sure that I express the gratitude of all servicemen with whom you have dealt, in sending this letter. I would appreciate it very much if you would convey to each member of your organization this expression of gratitude, so that they, too, may know of the appreciation of your splendid effort.[89]

While these letters were a wonderful and deserving acknowledgment of these women's work, the acknowledgment was not something they were seeking. The Malvern Hill Home Demonstration Club, which had many members who participated in Red Cross sewing, wrote in an article in 1942, "The chances are, at the end of this war, there will be no medals pinned on any of the members of the Malvern Hill Home Demonstration Club, but just the same they are out and out for the defense ... [to] do all it can to help make stronger this one link in Democracy's chain."[90] For the Committee on Civilian Defense in Newberry, South Carolina, another group whose members participated in Red Cross sewing, echoed these sentiments. In another 1942 article, they wrote, "All of us can't take part in the military defense of the Nation, but we are part of the military defense just the same. Before there can be victory, there must be toil and sacrifice. Every man, woman, and child best be ready to take his or her place."[91]

In American society during the 1940s, due to societal norms, everyone knew exactly where their place was. American women's place revolved around domesticity and the home, while men's lives revolved around work and providing for their families. While there were women who broke the mold and did war work to compensate for the men who left to go to war, the reality is most did not. Instead, when these homemakers, a term coined by Ladies Home Journal in the 1930s,[92] sewed for victory, they "still fit the guise of femininity because their actions were national fulfillment and not self-centered."[93] Without stepping outside of the gender norms and staying in their place, these women could aid the cause successfully and still receive recognition for their work. They proved that women could still be exactly what society asked of them, both pretty and patriotic.

About the Author

Aisha Manus is a part-time mermaid and a full-time cat lady who loves history. She has an MA in U.S. History, a BA in Asian and Pacific history, an AAS in Intelligence, and an AAS in Communication. Aisha is still in school, working on another degree or three. She is a disabled USAF veteran who dreams of being a professor when she grows up.

Bibliography

Newspapers

"1943 Jackson County Red Cross Production Report." The *Jackson Herald, Jefferson*, GA . February 10, 1944.

"31,280 Members of B'nai B'rith in Armed Force; 491 Killed or Missing and 466 Decorated, V-J Day Report Reveals." The *Southern Israelite*, VOL. XX-- No. 34, Atlanta, GA. August 27, 1945.

"4-H Members Here Did Outstanding Work During Year." The *Jackson Herald*, Jefferson, GA. November 19, 1942.

"4-H Members Here Did Outstanding Work During the Year." *The Forsyth County News*, Volume 34, Number 47. Cumming, GA. November 19, 1942.

"Around the Town: Incidents, Unusual and Ordinary, Gathers On Our Rounds." *The Clinton Chronicle*, Clinton, SC. February 11, 1943.

"Basque Frock." *The Jackson Herald*, Jefferson, GA. June 4, 1942.

Belk's. "National Sew and Save Week: February 21 to 28." *The Clinton Chronicle*, Clinton, SC. February 19, 1942.

Bigger, Virginia. "World War II Sewing Bee Keeps Women in Stitches Today." Washington, D.C: *NPR*, June 7, 1994.

Bryan, Mrs. Morris. "Report Jackson County Chapter Red Cross, 1942." *The Jackson Herald*, Jefferson, GA. April 22, 1943.

"Civilian Defense News: Red Cross Report." *Houston Home Journal*, VOL. LXXI, No. 41. Perry, Houston County, GA. October 8, 1942.

Counts, Ethel L. "H-D Column." *The Newberry Sun*, Newberry, SC: O.F. Armfield, Editor and Publisher. January 9, 1942.

Etheridge-Smith Company. "Now's the Time to Sew and Save." *The Jackson Progress-Argus*, Jackson, GA. February 24, 1944.

"Gate City Lodge, No. 144 Receives Service Flag." *The Southern Israelite*, Atlanta, GA. November 12, 1943.

"Good Management is Farm Women's Cheif War Role," *The Forsyth County News*, Cumming, GA. March 12, 1942.

"Hawthorn Garden Club Met Thursday with Mrs. Farley." *The Jackson Progress-Argus*, Jackson, GA. March 1, 1942.

"Hunter Field Commander Lauds Sewing Committee of Savannah USO-NCCS." *The Bulletin of the Catholic Laymen's Association of Georgia*, Augusta, GA. April 28, 1945.

"Jenkinsburg Garden Club." The Jackson Progress-Argus, Jackson, GA. October 15, 1942.

"Legion Auxiliary To Meet At Red Cross Room" *The Clinton Chronicle*, Clinton,

SC. February 11, 1943.

"Malvern Hill Club Makes Report." *The Camden Chronicle*, Camden, SC. April 10, 1942.

Moore, Bette Ann, ed. "Georgia Top 4-H'ers Win Trips to National Club Congress, Chicago." *The Forsyth County News*, Cumming, GA. November 25, 1943.

"Nearly All Red Cross Funds Go To Armed Forces: National Chapter Outlines How $200,000,000 Will Be Spent, War Activities to Get the Bulk." *The Jackson Progress-Argus*, Jackson, GA. March 16, 1944.

"News Summary of the Week in Georgia." *The Butler Herald*, Butler, GA. March 26, 1942.

"Page Three." *The Jackson Herald*, Jefferson, GA. March 12, 1942.

Pearson, Drew and Robert Allen. "Mrs. Woodrow Wilson." *The Sun*. Newberry, SC. March 13, 1942.

"Personal and Social Activities." *The Jackson Herald*, Jefferson, GA. March 19, 1942.

Powell, W.B. "Readers Write: Urgent Need for Scrap." *The Jackson Progress-Argus*, Jackson, GA. October 22, 1942.

"Red Cross News Items." *The Jackson Progress-Argus*, Jackson, GA. October 15, 1942.

"Red Cross News Items." *The Jackson Progress-Argus*, Jackson, GA. January 14, 1943.

"Red Cross News Items." *The Jackson Progress-Argus*, Jackson, GA. February 8, 1945.

"Red Cross Sewing Room At Augusta USO Club." *The Bulletin of the Catholic Laymen's Association of Georgia*, Augusta, GA. August 29, 1942.

"Red Cross Sewing Room Awaits Arrival of New Materials." *The Jackson Herald*, Jefferson, GA. February 26, 1942.

"Report of Red Cross Production Since 1940." *The Jackson Progress-Argus*, Jackson, GA. May 21, 1942.

"Robert Lurie Will Speak in Atlanta November 15." *The Southern Israelite*, Atlanta, GA. October 20, 1944.

"Sewing Contest Put on During Sew, Save Week: Girls Enter Any Garment They Wish; Style Show to be Given Wednesday." *The Bison,* Volume XIV—z24, Number 20. Harding College, Searcy, AK. March 3, 1942.

"U.D.C. Group Assists with Red Cross Work." *The Clinton Chronicle*, Clinton, SC., April 8, 1943.

UGA. "Red Cross Sends Out Call For University Volunteers." *The Red and Black,* VOL. L. NO. 2. The University of Georgia, Athens, GA. June 23, 1944.

U.S. Treasury Department. "Style with Thrift For War Bonds." *The Jackson Herald*, Jefferson, GA. October 4, 1944.

VonTresckow, Sadie K. "Red Cross Notes," *The Camden Chronicle,* Camden, SC. June 11, 1943.

VonTresckow, Sadie K. "Red Cross Notes," *The Camden Chronicle,* Camden, SC. May 26, 1944.

"Woman 92 Knits for Soldiers," *The Jackson Progress-Argus*, Jackson, GA. July 16, 1942.

Books/ Journals

Babic, Annessa Ann. *America's Changing Icon: Constructing Patriotic Women from World War I to the Present.* Lanham, MD: Fairleigh Dickinson University Press, 2018.

Brackman, Barbara. *Quilts from the Civil War. Nine Projects, Historic Notes, Diary Entries.* Lafayette, CA: C&T Publishing, Inc. 2009.

Brock, Julia, Dickey, Jennifer W., Harker, Richard, and Lewis, Catherine. *Beyond Rosie: A Documentary History of Women and World War II.* Fayetteville: University of Arkansas Press, 2015.

Cox, Karen. *Dixie's Daughters: The United Daughters of the Confederacy and the Preservation of Confederate Culture.* Gainsville, FL: University Press of Florida, 2004.

Duntz, Gertrude C. "She Saves Who Sews: For Victory" Book No. 250, Shelby, NC:

Lily Mills Company, 1942.

Gundersen, Joan R. *To Be Useful To the World: Women in Revolutionary America, 1740-1790*. New York, NY: Twayne Publishers, 1996.

Hall, Martha L, Belinda T Orzada, and Dilia Lopez-Gydosh. "American Women's Wartime Dress: Sociocultural Ambiguity Regarding Women's Roles During World War II." The Journal of American Culture 38, no. 3 (September 2015): 232–242.

"Make and Mend: For Victory" Book No. S-10, USA: The Spool Cotton Company, 1942.

Springate, Megan E. "Material Drives on the World War II Home Front (U.S. National Park Service)." National Parks Service. Accessed October 11, 2023. https://www.nps.gov/articles/000/material-drives-on-the-world-war-ii-home-front.htm.

Ulrich, Laurel Thatcher. *The Age of Homespun: Objects and Stories in the Creation of an American Myth*. Knopf Doubleday Publishing Group, 2009.

Ulrich, Laurel Thatcher. "Vertuous Women Found: New England Ministerial Literature, 1668-1735." American Quarterly, Vol. 28, No. 1 (Spring, 1976): 20–40. Accessed at https://doi.org/10.2307/2712475

Witkowski, Terrence H. "World War II Poster Campaigns—Preaching Frugality to American Consumers." *Journal of Advertising* 32, no. 1 (April 1, 2003): 69–82.

Yellin, Emily. *Our Mothers' War: American Women at Home and at the Front During World War II*. New York, NY: Free Press, 2004.

Photographs/ Posters

Collins, Majory. "New York, New York. The War Emergency Board of the Fur Industry Formed A Fur Vest Project. Various Fur Factories Donate the Services of Their Employees One Day A Week to Make Fur-lined Vests for the Merchant Marines. The Fur Is All From Voluntary Donations From the Public. Workers Sewing Together the Outside of the Vest Which is Made of Heavy Cotton material." Library of Congress, Prints & Photographs Division, FSA/OWI Collection, Reproduction Number: LC-USW3-013077-D (b&w film neg.), December 1942, Accessed at https://www.loc.gov/pictures/item/2017841462/

"Cynthia Stitches Basic Seams Before Fitting, A Principle of Simplified Sewing. While No New Sewing Machines Are Being Made and the Factories Are Turning Out War Goods WPB (War Production Board) Assures An Adequate Supply of

Machine Repair Parts For Home Dressmakers. To fully Utilize Existing Machines, Many Women Form Community Pools, Make Machines Available to Those Who Would Like to Buy Them and Can't." Library of Congress, Prints & Photographs Division, FSA/OWI Collection, Reproduction Number: LC-USW33-021689-ZC (b&w film neg.) 1943. Accessed at https://www.loc.gov/pictures/item/2017877144/

"Discarded Stockings Go to War. Sewing Primer Caps for Powder Bags From Cloth Made of Discarded Silk Stockings. Fifteen Pairs of Old Stockings Provide Sufficient Cloth for an Average-Size Powder Bag" Library of Congress, Prints & Photographs Division, FSA/OWI Collection, Reproduction Number: LC-USE6-D-007432 (b&w film neg.), December 1942. Accessed at https://www.loc.gov/pictures/item/2017695011/

Pistchal. "Sew for Victory." Federal Arts Project, New York, NY: N.Y.C. W.P.A. War Services, 1941. https://www.loc.gov/pictures/item/98516630/

Red Cross. "National Sew and Save Week" Stamps. O.P.A., 1939–1945.

Rosener, Ann. " Glendale, Calif. March 1943. American Women Volunteer Service 'Button Brigade' Sewing On Corporal's Chevron and Mending A Ripped Shirt Seam in the U.S. Army Air Force Barracks." Library of Congress, Prints & Photographs Division, FSA/OWI Collection, Reproduction Number:---, March 1943. Accessed at https://www.loc.gov/pictures/item/2005675102/

"Wartime Conservation Through Home Sewing is Demonstrated by Powers Model Cynthia Hope Who Works With A Fabric-Saving Dress Pattern. All Patterns Are Now Adjusted to WPB (War Production Board) Conservation Rules. Average Saving: 1/8 Yard Per Dress. Cynthia Cuts The Top of Her Contrast Dress with A Remnant Which Would Otherwise Be Wasted. Utilizing Remnants Saves Tremendous Yardage, Gets Smart Results." Library of Congress, Prints & Photographs Division, FSA/OWI Collection, Reproduction Number: LC-USW33-021690-ZC (b&w film neg.) 1943. Accessed at https://www.loc.gov/pictures/item/2017877145/

Dissertations and Theses

Dalton, Lauren, Pauline Sullivan, Jeanne Heitmeyer, and Ann DuPont. "Robertson's Model: A Framework for Exploration of World War II Conservation Consumption Policy Influence on Fashion in the US." *International Journal of Consumer* Studies 36, no. 6 (November 2012): 611–621.

Jurkola, Johanna M. "Treading Lightly on the Environment: Using Second World War Fabric Saving and Clothing Reuse Techniques to Inform Contemporary

Women's Clothing Design." Order No. MQ87792, University of Alberta (Canada), 2003. https://search-proquest-com.ezproxy1.apus.edu/docview/305251395?accountid=8289.

Moskowitz, Daniel B. "HEMMED IN." *World War II* 32, no. 6 (04, 2018): 62. https://search-proquest-com.ezproxy1.apus.edu/docview/1991143281?accountid=8289.

Mower, Jennifer M. "Pretty and Patriotic": Women's Consumption of Apparel During World War II. : Oregon State University. https://ir.library.oregonstate.edu/concern/graduate_thesis_or_dissertations/b5644v40p

Endnotes

1   Laurel Thatcher Ulrich. "Vertuous Women Found: New England Ministerial Literature, 1668-1735." *American Quarterly*, Vol. 28, No. 1 (Spring, 1976), https://doi.org/10.2307/2712475. 20

2   Joan R. Gundersen. *To Be Useful To the World: Women in Revolutionary America, 1740-1790.* (New York, NY: Twayne Publishers, 1996), 173.

3   Laurel Thatcher Ulrich. *The Age of Homespun: Objects and Stories in the Creation of an American Myth.* (Knopf Doubleday Publishing Group, 2009), 178.

4   Barbara Brackman. *Quilts from the Civil War. Nine Projects, Historic Notes, Diary Entries.* (Lafayette, CA: C&T Publishing, Inc., 2009), 53.

5   "Woman 92 Knits for Soldiers," *The Jackson Progress-Argus*, Jackson, GA. July 16, 1942.

6   Jennifer M. Mower. "'Pretty and Patriotic': Women's Consumption of Apparel During World War II." Oregon State University. https://ir.library.oregonstate.edu/concern/graduate_thesis_or_dissertations/b5644v40p. 44.

7   Daniel B. Moskowitz. "HEMMED IN." *World War II* 32, no. 6 (04, 2018): 62. https://search-proquest-com.ezproxy1.apus.edu/docview/1991143281?accountid=8289. 66.

8   "Cynthia stitches basic seams before fitting, a principle of simplified sewing. While no new sewing machines are being made and the factories are turning out war goods (WPB (War Production Board) assures an adequate supply of machine repair parts for home dressmakers. To fully utilize existing machines, many women form community pools, make machines available to those who would like to buy them and can't." Library of Congress, Prints & Photographs Division, FSA/OWI Collection, Reproduction Number: LC-USW33-021689-ZC (b&w film neg.) 1943. Accessed https://www.loc.gov/pictures/item/2017877144/

9   "Nearly All Red Cross Funds Go To Armed Forces: National Chapter Outlines How

$200,000,000 Will Be Spent, War Activities to Get the Bulk." *The Jackson Progress-Argus*, Jackson, GA. March 16, 1944.

10 Sadie K. VonTresckow. "Red Cross Notes," *The Camden Chronicle*, Camden, SC. June 11, 1943.

11 Sadie K. VonTresckow. "Red Cross Notes," *The Camden Chronicle*, Camden, SC. May 26, 1944.

12 "Report of Red Cross Production Since 1940." *The Jackson Progress-Argus*, Jackson, GA. May 21, 1942.

13 "Red Cross News Items." *The Jackson Progress-Argus*, Jackson, GA. January 14, 1943.

14 "Red Cross News Items." *The Jackson Progress-Argus*, Jackson, GA. February 8, 1945.

15 Mrs. Morris Bryan. "Report Jackson County Chapter Red Cross, 1942." *The Jackson Herald*, Jefferson, GA. April 22, 1943.

16 "Red Cross Sewing Room Awaits Arrival of New Materials." *The Jackson Herald*, Jefferson, GA. February 26, 1942.

17 "Personal and Social Activities." *The Jackson Herald*, Jefferson, GA. March 19, 1942.

18 "1943 Jackson County Red Cross Production Report." *The Jackson Herald*, Jefferson, GA. February 10, 1944.

19 "Civilian Defense News: Red Cross Report." *Houston Home Journal*, VOL. LXXI, No. 41. Perry, Houston County, GA. October 8, 1942.

20 UGA. "Red Cross Sends Out Call For University Volunteers." *The Red and Black*, VOL. L. NO. 2. The University of Georgia, Athens, GA. June 23, 1944.

21 Terrence H. Witkowski. "World War II Poster Campaigns--Preaching Frugality to American Consumers." *Journal of Advertising* 32, no. 1 (April 1, 2003: 69–82), 71.

22 Martha L. Hall, Belinda T Orzada, and Dilia Lopez-Gydosh. "American Women's Wartime Dress: Sociocultural Ambiguity Regarding Women's Roles During World War II." *The Journal of American Culture* 38, no. 3 (September 2015: 232–242), 234.

23 Terrence H. Witkowski. "World War II Poster Campaigns," 72.

24 Pistchal. *Sew for Victory*. Federal Arts Project, New York, NY: N.Y.C. W.P.A. War Services, 1941. https://www.loc.gov/pictures/item/98516630/

25 Julia Brock, Dickey, Jennifer W., Harker, Richard, and Lewis, Catherine. *Beyond Rosie: A Documentary History of Women and World War II*. (Fayetteville: University of Arkansas Press, 2015), 124.

26 Pistchal. *Sew for Victory*. 1941.

27 Terrence H. Witkowski. "World War II Poster Campaigns," 73.

28 Ibid., 75.

29 W.B. Powell. "Readers Write: Urgent Need for Scrap." *The Jackson Progress-Argus*, Jackson, GA. October 22, 1942.

30 Red Cross. "National Sew and Save Week" Stamps. O.P.A., 1939–1945.

31 Belk's. "National Sew and Save Week: February 21 to 28." *The Clinton Chronicle*, Clinton, SC. February 19, 1942.

32 Etheridge-Smith Company. "Now's the Time to Sew and Save." The Jackson Progress-Argus, Jackson, GA., February 24, 1944.

33 Martha L. Hall, Belinda T Orzada, and Dilia Lopez-Gydosh. "American Women's Wartime Dress," 234.

34 Daniel B. Moskowitz. "HEMMED IN," 65.

35 "Good Management is Farm Women's Cheif War Role," *The Forsyth County News,* Cumming, GA. March 12, 1942.

36 Johanna M. Jurkola. "Treading Lightly on the Environment: Using Second World War Fabric Saving and Clothing Reuse Techniques to Inform Contemporary Women's Clothing Design." Order No. MQ87792, University of Alberta (Canada), 2003. (https://search-proquest- com.ezproxy1.apus.edu/docview/305251395?accountid=8289.) 96.

37 Gertrude C. Duntz. "She Who Save Sews - For Victory" Book No. 250 (Shelby, NC: Lily Mills Company, 1942), 3.

38 Virginia Bigger. "World War II Sewing Bee Keeps Women in Stitches Today." Washington, D.C: NPR, June 7, 1994.

39 Karen Cox. *Dixie's Daughters: The United Daughters of the Confederacy and the Preservation of Confederate Culture.* (Gainsville, FL: University Press of Florida, 2004), 155–157.

40 "Around the Town: Incidents, Unusual and Ordinary, Gathers On Our Rounds." *The Clinton Chronicle*, Clinton, SC. February 11, 1943.

41 "U.D.C. Group Assists with Red Cross Work." *The Clinton Chronicle,* Clinton, SC. April 8, 1943.

42 Emily Yellin. *Our Mothers' War,* 168.

43 "Legion Auxiliary To Meet At Red Cross Room" *The Clinton Chronicle*, Clinton, SC. February 11, 1943.

44 "4-H Members Here Did Outstanding Work During Year" *The Jackson Herald*, Jefferson, GA. November 19, 1942.

45 "4-H Members Here Did Outstanding Work During the Year." *The Forsyth County News*, Volume 34, Number 47. Cumming, GA. November 19, 1942.

46 "Red Cross News Items." *The Jackson Progress-Argus*, Jackson, GA. October 15, 1942.

47 "Jenkinsburg Garden Club." *The Jackson Progress-Argus,* Jackson, GA. October 15, 1942.

48 "Hawthorn Garden Club Met Thursday with Mrs. Farley." *The Jackson Progress-Argus,* Jackson, GA. March 1, 1942.

49 Emily Yellin. *Our Mothers' War,* 345.

50 "Robert Lurie Will Speak in Atlanta November 15." *The Southern Israelite,* Atlanta, GA. October 20, 1944.

51 "31,280 Members of B'nai B'rith in Armed Force; 491 Killed or Missing and 466 Decorated, V-J Day Report Reveals." *The Southern Israelite,* VOL. XX-- No. 34, Atlanta, GA., August 27, 1945.

52 "Gate City Lodge, No. 144 Receives Service Flag." *The Southern Israelite,* Atlanta, GA. November 12, 1943.

53 Drew Pearson and Robert Allen. "Mrs. Woodrow Wilson." *The Sun.* Newberry, SC. March 13, 1942.

54 Daniel B. Moskowitz. "HEMMED IN," 64.

55 "Page Three." *The Jackson Herald,* Jefferson, GA. March 12, 1942.

56 "Red Cross Sewing Room At Augusta USO Club." *The Bulletin of the Catholic Laymen's Association of Georgia,* Augusta, GA. August 29, 1942.

57 Ann Rosener. "Glendale, Calif. March 1943. American Women Volunteer Service 'Button Brigade' Sewing on corporal's chevron and mending a ripped shirt seam in the U.S. Army air force barracks." Library of Congress, Prints & Photographs Division, FSA/OWI Collection, Reproduction Number:---, March 1943. Accessed at https://www.loc.gov/pictures/item/2005675102/

58 Emily Yellin. *Our Mothers' War,* 176.

59 Ibid., 169.

60 "News Summary of the Week in Georgia." *The Butler Herald,* Butler, GA. March 26, 1942.

61 "Hunter Field Commander Lauds Sewing Committee of Savannah USO-NCCS." *The Bulletin of the Catholic Laymen's Association of Georgia*, Augusta, GA. April 28, 1945.

62 Daniel B. Moskowitz. "HEMMED IN," 64.

63 Jennifer M. Mower. "Pretty and Patriotic," 1-2.

64 "Discarded stockings go to war. Sewing primer caps for powder bags from cloth made of discarded silk stockings. Fifteen pairs of old stockings provide sufficient cloth for an

average-size powder bag" Library of Congress, Prints & Photographs Division, FSA/OWI Collection, Reproduction Number: LC-USE6-D-007432 (b&w film neg.), December 1942. Accessed at https://www.loc.gov/pictures/item/2017695011/

65 Megan E Springate, "Material Drives on the World War II Home Front (U.S. National Park Service)," National Parks Service, accessed October 11, 2023, https://www.nps.gov/articles/000/material-drives-on-the-world-war-ii-home-front.htm.

66 Jennifer M. Mower. "Pretty and Patriotic," 45.

67 Daniel B. Moskowitz. "HEMMED IN," 64.

68 Martha L. Hall, Belinda T Orzada, and Dilia Lopez-Gydosh. "American Women's Wartime Dress," 240.

69 Jennifer M. Mower. "Pretty and Patriotic," 18-19.

70 Johanna M. Jurkola. "Treading Lightly on the Environment," 107.

71 Jennifer M. Mower. "Pretty and Patriotic," 22.

72 "Wartime conservation through home sewing is demonstrated by Powers model Cynthia Hope who works with a fabric-saving dress pattern. All patterns are now adjusted to WPB (War Production Board) conservation rules. Average saving: 1/8 yard per dress. Cynthia cuts the top of her contrast dress with a remnant which would otherwise be wasted. Utilizing remnants saves tremendous yardage, gets smart results." Library of Congress, Prints & Photographs Division, FSA/OWI Collection, Reproduction Number: LC-USW33-021690-ZC (b&w film neg.) 1943. Accessed at https://www.loc.gov/pictures/item/2017877145/

73 "Basque Frock." *The Jackson Herald*, Jefferson, GA. June 4, 1942.

74 U.S. Treasury Department. "Style with Thrift For War Bonds." *The Jackson Herald,* Jefferson, GA. October 4, 1944.

75 Gertrude C. Duntz. "She Who Save Sews - For Victory," 7.

76 "Make and Mend: For Victory," Book No. S-10, (USA: The Spool Cotton Company, 1942), 38.

77 Ibid., 2.

78 Jennifer M. Mower. "Pretty and Patriotic," 75.

79 Johanna M. Jurkola. "Treading Lightly on the Environment," 108.

80 Daniel B. Moskowitz. „HEMMED IN," 65.

81 Jennifer M. Mower. "Pretty and Patriotic," 79.

82 Ibid., 114.

83 Daniel B. Moskowitz. "HEMMED IN," 65.

84 Bette Ann Moore, ed. "Georgia Top 4-H'ers Win Trips to National Club Congress, Chicago." *The Forsyth County News,* Cumming, GA. November 25, 1943.

85 Jennifer M. Mower. "Pretty and Patriotic," 88.

86 "Sewing Contest Put on During Sew, Save Week: Girls Enter Any Garment They Wish; Style Show to be Given Wednesday." *The Bison,* Volume XIV—z24, Number 20. Harding College, Searcy, AK. March 3, 1942.

87 "Around the Town: Incidents, Unusual and Ordinary, Gathers On Our Rounds." *The Clinton Chronicle*, Clinton, SC. February 11, 1943.

88 Sadie K. VonTresckow. "Red Cross Notes," *The Camden Chronicle*, Camden, SC, June 11, 1943.

89 "Hunter Field Commander Lauds Sewing Committee of Savannah USO-NCCS." *The Bulletin of the Catholic Laymen's Association of Georgia*, Augusta, GA. April 28, 1945.

90 "Malvern Hill Club Makes Report," *The Camden Chronicle,* Camden, SC. April 10, 1942.

91 Ethel L. Counts. "H-D Column." *The Newberry Sun*, Newberry, SC: O.F. Armfield, Editor and Publisher. January 9, 1942

92 Martha L. Hall, Belinda T Orzada, and Dilia Lopez-Gydosh. "American Women's Wartime Dress," 233.

93 Annessa Ann Babic. *America's Changing Icon: Constructing Patriotic Women from World War I to the Present.* (Lanham, MD: Fairleigh Dickinson University Press, 2018), 65.

The Guadalcanal Campaign: A Historiographical Essay

William F. Lawson

Liberty University

ABSTRACT

The Guadalcanal Campaign of 1942–1943 was the Allies' first offensive in World War II. The First Marine Division landing in the Solomon Islands kicked-off the long road to Tokyo and victory in the Pacific. The ensuing six-month campaign was unequaled for sustained violence at sea, on land, and in the air. The decisive nature of the campaign and the three-dimensional (land, sea, and air) aspects of the combat inspired a myriad of scholarly and popular histories, biographies, monographs, and novels.

Keywords: Historiography, World War II, Pacific War, Guadalcanal, United States Marine Corps, United States Army

La campaña de Guadalcanal: un ensayo historiográfico

RESUMEN

La campaña de Guadalcanal de 1942-1943 fue la primera ofensiva de los aliados en la Segunda Guerra Mundial. El desembarco de la Primera División de Infantería de Marina en las Islas Salomón inició el largo camino hacia Tokio y la victoria en el Pacífico. La campaña de seis meses que siguió fue inigualable por la violencia sostenida en el mar, la tierra y el aire. La naturaleza decisiva de la campaña y los aspectos tridimensionales (tierra, mar y aire) del combate inspiraron una gran cantidad de historias, biografías, monografías y novelas académicas y populares.

Palabras clave: Historiografía, Segunda Guerra Mundial, Guerra del Pacífico, Guadalcanal, Cuerpo de Marines de los Estados Unidos, Ejército de los Estados Unidos

doi: 10.18278/mhc.1.2.4

瓜达尔卡纳尔岛战役：一篇史学史论文

摘要

1942年至1943年的瓜达尔卡纳尔岛战役是盟军在第二次世界大战中的第一次攻势。美国海军陆战队第一师在所罗门群岛登陆，打开了通往东京和太平洋胜利的漫长道路。随后的六个月战役无论是在海上、陆地、还是空中，都发生了前所未有的持续暴力事件。这次战役的关键性质和战斗的三个维度（陆地、海上和空中）激发了无数的学术史、通俗史、传记、专著以及小说。

关键词：史学史，第二次世界大战，太平洋战争，瓜达尔卡纳尔岛，美国海军陆战队，美国陆军

The Guadalcanal Campaign of 1942–1943 is, quite literally, legendary. The United States First Marine Division's landing at Guadalcanal and Tulagi in the Solomon Islands was America's first offensive action of World War II. Sandwiched between the Battle of Midway and the Allied invasion of North Africa, the gripping struggle for Guadalcanal led the headlines of U.S. newspapers for nearly four months. It was a campaign of attrition encompassing all three dimensions of warfare: land, air, and sea. Before it was done, the six-month campaign witnessed eight major naval engagements; multiple land battles involving two Marine and two U.S. Army infantry divisions; and almost daily air battles fought between Guadalcanal's "Cactus Air Force," and the Japanese. Those six months also witnessed a staggering bloodletting, with Japanese fatalities on land, sea, and in the air totaling at least 30,343, while the Allies lost 7,100 men killed.

Fittingly, the literature on Guadalcanal is massive, ranging from official histories to memoirs. This essay cannot possibly chronicle them all. The author has, therefore, selected the major works across that spectrum covering the arc of scholarship regarding the campaign as well as the notable works of memory. The discussion will include campaign monographs, theater histories, and one notable general history.

Guadalcanal held such a central place in the minds of Americans that the first accounts appeared within months of the island's final conquest in February 1943. The first and best regarded was *Guadalcanal Diary* by war correspondent Richard Tregaskis, published in November 1943. Tregaskis landed with the Marines on August 7, 1942, and chronicled his experiences until his departure on September 25. Noted for its gritty detail, *Guadalcanal Diary* has been cited numerous times

First Marine Division landing on Guadalcanal – August 7, 1942. The Guadalcanal Campaign (August 1942 to February 1943) was the Allies' first offensive in WWII. The Marine landings kicked off the long road to Tokyo and victory in the Pacific. The ensuing six-month campaign was unequaled for sustained violence at sea, on land, and in the air. (National Archives).

and is still lauded for its accuracy almost eighty years later. Tregaskis is widely recognized for his outstanding first-hand accounts from World War II through Vietnam.

One other wartime publication deserves mention here: *The Island* (1944), by First Marine Division public affairs officer Captain Herbert Merillat. Another detailed and well-written account, Merillat draws on official records and first-hand experience to document the First Marine Division's operations, from shipping out to the Pacific in May 1942 to its withdrawal from combat in December of that year. Being published so early, the work lacks a larger context beyond its focus on the First Marine Division, but it complements later, more general works with its focus. Like *Guadalcanal Diary*, *The Island* serves as a rich source material for later historians. Merillat himself used his earlier work for the well-received memoir *Guadalcanal Remembered* (1982), which provides more context for the campaign and, like *The Island*, serves modern historians as a solid source.

The sheer number of memoirists from Guadalcanal demands judicious parsing. Two others merit inclusion: Robert Leckie's *Helmet for My Pillow* (1957) and Merrill B. Twining and Neil G. Carey's *No Bended Knee: The Battle for Guadalcanal* (1996). Leckie's is justly among the most famous memoirs in military history. Employing eloquent prose, the author recounts a hard-hitting account from the viewpoint of a Marine private in his first combat action. A reporter before the war, Leckie writes with unsparing authority on the brutality of war and muses on why men fight.

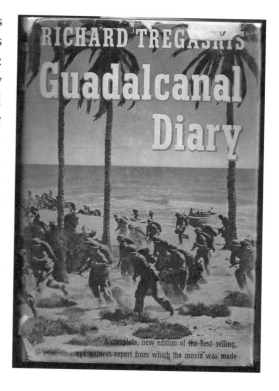

Twining tells his story from the command structure's other end. Twining was the First Marine Division's operations officer and had first-hand experience with the division's planning and execution of combat actions and more mundane activities. There is nothing particularly revelatory about the book, but it confirms some aspects of earlier accounts and has provided source material for several well-received later works, as has *Helmet for My Pillow.*

The U.S. Navy's Office of Naval Intelligence published monographs addressing the campaign's several phases, beginning in 1943. These works were initially classified, though they later became publicly available. *The Landing in the Solomons, 7-8 August 1942* (1943); *The Battle of Savo Island, 9 August 1942* (1943); *Battle of Cape Esperance, 11 October 1942; Battle of Santa Cruz Islands, 26 October 1942* (1943); *Battle of Guadalcanal, 11-15 November 1942* (1944); and *Battle of Tassafaronga, 30 November 1942;* and *Japanese Evacuation of*

Guadalcanal, Including the Loss of the Chicago, 29 January-8 February 1943 (1944) are straightforward recitations of the actions in question with little to no placement of the campaign in greater context. Since they were published during the war, there is no discussion of the Japanese side other than what was observed by the American servicemen involved.

The campaign's first scholarly treatment appeared in 1948 as Volume V of the distinguished Harvard historian Samuel Eliot Morison's *History of United States Naval Operations in World War II. The Struggle for Guadalcanal, August 1942–February 1943*, is still considered the definitive account by many. Morison was commissioned into the Navy by President Franklin D. Roosevelt to chronicle the naval war and was present for part of the campaign. He also had full access to participants and all official naval and Marine records. Morison, who by the end of the war was a vice admiral, was the first to begin placing the campaign in context, though even he stopped short of calling it the decisive battle of the Pacific War. Guadalcanal's decisive nature is now the general historical consensus.

The U.S. Army and Marine Corps followed with official histories in 1949 and 1958, respectively. *Guadalcanal: The First Offensive, The United States Army in World War II: The War in the Pacific* and *Pearl Harbor to Guadalcanal: History of U.S. Marine Corps Operations in World War II, Volume I* are well-researched but limited in scope as they, understandably, focus on the contributions of the respective services for which they were written.

Samuel B. Griffith, a Marine battalion commander on Guadalcanal, made the next major scholarly contribution to the campaign's literature with *The Battle for Guadalcanal* (1963). Griffith combined first-hand insight with access to most of the major players on the American side, including both ground force commanders and several members of their respective staffs. He also used official records and was the first to incorporate the Japanese side of events through correspondence with soldiers who had served in the campaign, as well as the Japanese War Ministry's history section. Griffith was among the first to name Guadalcanal as the Pacific War's turning point, though he still lumped it alongside Midway and the 1944 Mariana Islands Campaign in that regard. The slow change of that view will be addressed later. New access to Japanese views on the campaign's impact on their ability to prosecute the war led to recognition of Guadalcanal's true importance.

Robert Leckie contributed a second Guadalcanal account in 1965 with *Challenge for the Pacific: Guadalcanal: The Turning Point of the War*. This new effort had the advantage of research beyond Leckie's immediate experiences and discussed the entire campaign, including the Japanese side. Leckie's battle accounts are among the genre's best, and one sees Griffith's influence in his overall conclusions. Though not a professional historian, Leckie went farther than Griffith to declare Guadalcanal, not Midway, as the Pacific War's turning point. Modern historians recognize that Midway provided strategic parity in the Pacific, with Guadalcanal throwing the initiative squarely to the American side. Leckie was a leader in advancing this distinction.

Thomas G. Miller's popular history of Guadalcanal's air war, *The Cactus Air Force* (1969), wrapped up the major works of the 1960s. Miller recounts the harrowing struggle of the Marine, Army, and Navy pilots fighting to protect the combat troops and their naval lifeline as well as deny Japanese reinforcements to their island garrison. *The Cactus Air Force* is still considered the best single account of the campaign's crucial air component.

Serious studies of the Guadalcanal Campaign waned as the more spectacular victory at Midway garnered most of the attention as the Pacific turning point. Guadalcanal did figure prominently in John Toland's Pulitzer Prize-winning *The Rising Sun: The Decline and Fall of the Japanese Empire, 1936–1945* (1970), the first English language account of the Japanese side of the war. But Toland stopped short of declaring it the turning point. He did, however, reference Major General Kiyotake Kawaguchi, who commanded the first Japanese attempt to eject the First Marine Division from the island. Immediately after the Japanese evacuation, Kawaguchi flatly stated, "We lost the battle, and Japan lost the war."

Ronald Spector's *Eagle Against the Sun: The American War with Japan* (1985) is generally considered the best

single-volume work on the Pacific War. As such, Guadalcanal receives its share of ink. Interestingly, Spector acknowledges Guadalcanal's role as the first Allied offensive but characterizes it as a defensive victory. He was among the first to place Guadalcanal in the larger context of the attritional Solomons and New Guinea Campaigns, which proved to be the ruin of Japanese naval aviation as well as a large portion of the Imperial Army.

Richard B. Frank's *Guadalcanal: The Definitive Account of the Landmark Battle* (1990) was the first major book-length work on the campaign since the mid-1960s. Frank is not a professional historian, but his meticulously researched work broke new ground and set the tone for later works on the subject. Frank worked with a translator to examine numerous previously untapped Japanese primary sources and provided exhaustive data on Guadalcanal and its Pacific War significance.

Frank notes that, strategically, Midway and Guadalcanal often seem to blend, but the data regarding the nature of the casualties (Japan lost most of its veteran pilots and aircrews in the Solomons), material losses, and Japan's comparative ability to make good those losses, show Guadalcanal to have been the war's decisive campaign. As noted, this is now the accepted view among modern historians. An interview with a Japanese naval officer confirms the view of Guadalcanal as the war's turning point while acknowledging the importance of Midway: "There are many famous battles in the war—Saipan, Leyte,

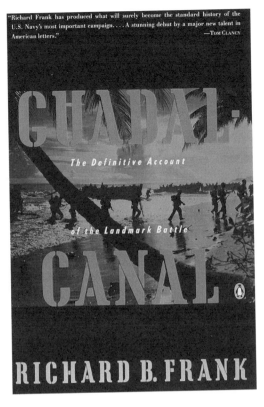

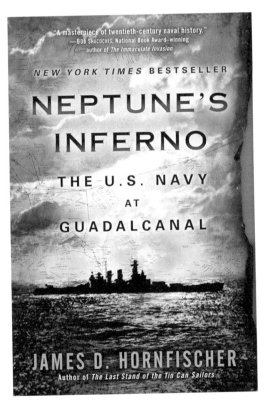

Okinawa, etc. But after the war, we [the professional military] talked only about two, Midway and Guadalcanal." Frank's book contains detailed notes but, disappointingly, does not contain a bibliography.

Franks' conclusions regarding Guadalcanal were echoed in what is currently the definitive work on the Japanese Navy at Midway, Jonathan Parshall and Anthony Tully's *Shattered Sword: The Untold Story of the Battle of Midway* (2005). Addressing the issue in the context of Midway, the authors, sourcing Frank, among others, demonstrate that Midway was not the decisive battle of the Pacific War, and apply that tag to Guadalcanal and the Solomons Campaign as a whole.

The second decade of the twenty-first century saw a flurry of works on the Pacific War, with Guadalcanal getting its fair share of attention. First was naval historian James D. Hornfischer's *Neptune's Inferno: The U.S. Navy at Guadalcanal* (2011). As noted previously, Guadalcanal was truly a three-dimensional campaign where the failure of one dimension (land, air, or sea) would have doomed the entire enterprise. Such a phenomenon provides ample opportunity for a wide range of approaches, in this case, a deep look at the naval engagements that kept the supply lines open for the Marines on the ground.

Neptune's Inferno combines the readability of popular history with the scholarship of academic research. Guadalcanal was literally the training ground for the U.S. surface fleet. Painful and deadly lessons were learned, which carried over to the rest of the war and beyond. Radar made its first contribution to surface warfare, and the U.S. Navy learned how to fight at night. Once again, Hornfischer brings the Guadalcanal campaign into clearer focus regarding its impact on the entire war.

The second installment of Ian W. Toll's Pacific War Trilogy, *The Conquering Tide: War in the Pacific Islands, 1942–1944*, was published in 2015. Though Toll's work has a theater-wide focus, Guadalcanal features prominently in the narrative, which echoes the now familiar theme of Guadalcanal as the war's turning point. Like Hornfischer, Toll combines outstanding scholarship with riveting first-hand accounts of sailors, airmen, soldiers, and Marines. It is easily one of the most readable accounts of the war.

Journalist Joseph Wheelan turned out the first comprehensive book on Guadalcanal since Frank with *Midnight in the Pacific: Guadalcanal-The World War II Battle that Turned the Tide of War* (2017). Despite the cumbersome title, Wheelan produced an accessible, reader-friendly, and factually accurate popular history. The work's chronological narrative approach is a strength, helping readers properly place events in space and time.

The final well-done popular study to be discussed is the two-part examination of the battle by Jeffrey Cox, *Morning Star, Midnight Sun: The Early Guadalcanal-Solomons Campaign of World War II, August-October 1942* (2018) and *Blazing Star, Setting Sun:*

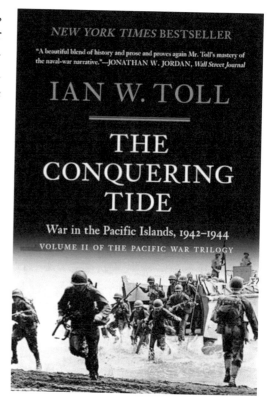

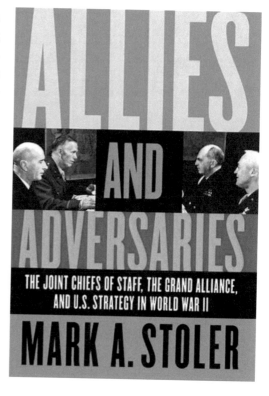

The Conclusion of the Guadalcanal-Solomons Campaign of World War II, November 1942–March 1943 (2020). Rich in detail, Cox makes good use of Japanese sources to fill out his narrative. The works are very readable, but a weakness is the lack of regional maps, which is really a necessity in a campaign history, especially one in which the general reader is probably unfamiliar with the geography.

The most scholarly study of the decade, perhaps the most scholarly since Morison, is Sean M. Judge's *The Turn of the Tide in the Pacific War: Strategic Initiative, Intelligence, and Command, 1941–1943* (2018). This innovative work examines strategic initiative's elusive nature and applies it to the Pacific War's crucial first year. While the fact that Guadalcanal was the war's turning point is now firmly established, in the macro sense, Judge is the first to dig deeply into why the initiative swung as it did. He also ties the Guadalcanal and New Guinea Campaigns irrevocably together as mutually supporting and influential. The work is a fascinating academic study that dramatically advances our understanding of Guadalcanal.

Two specialized works deserve mention, as they deal with certain aspects of the campaign. Jeter A. Isely and Philip A. Crowl's *The U.S. Marines and Amphibious War* (1951) is still a touchstone work chronicling the development and application of amphibious warfare as practiced by the Marine Corps. While the Marines landed unopposed on Guadalcanal, the campaign taught valuable lessons about supporting an amphibious expeditionary force in terms of logistics and fire support.

Guadalcanal demonstrated the absolute necessity of "combat loading" transport ships to facilitate the combat effectiveness of the troops ashore, as well as importance of the constant presence of the support fleet to morale among those troops. Furthermore, those same troops proved vulnerable to Japanese night naval actions, reinforcing the need to provide a fleet to shield them. Interestingly, the authors quote a Japanese naval planner as saying, "After Guadalcanal, in the latter part of 1942, I felt we could not win." They further quote a Japanese Army General Staff officer who said, "As for the turning point (of the war), when the positive action ceased or even became negative, it was, I feel, at Guadalcanal." It seems the Japanese recognized Guadalcanal's strategic importance before the Americans did.

Mark A. Stoler's outstanding command study, *Allies and Adversaries, The Joint Chiefs of Staff, The Grand Alliance, and U.S. Strategy in World War II* (2000), provides keen insight into the decision to strike at Guadalcanal when commanders in the Pacific believed that offensive action was not yet possible. The decision challenged the agreed-upon "Germany-first" strategy and was disputed at the highest levels. Stoler skillfully parses the intricate negotiations and machinations that eventually led to the Marine landings on August 7, 1942.

Finally, this discussion would not be complete without Gerhard Weinberg's monumental *A World at Arms: A Global History of World War II* (1995-2005). Quite probably the finest single-volume history of the Second World War, its great strength is placing each event in context to provide a truly global perspective. Weinberg relates how the Guadalcanal Campaign was partially aimed at deterring a Japanese attack on the Soviet Union, a concept echoed by Stoler, at a critical time during the war in Russia.

The Battles of Guadalcanal and Stalingrad were fought almost exactly in time with each other, and both proved to be major milestones on the road to an eventual Allied victory. The campaign's attritional nature also shut down any hope the Japanese may have held for linking up with Germany in the Middle East or South Asia. Weinberg is quite clear about Guadalcanal's importance, not only in the Pacific, but globally.

Befitting its importance, the Guadalcanal Campaign is richly chronicled and interest in this decisive event seems as strong as ever. Pacific War literature has enjoyed a renaissance in the last decade. As the language barrier is slowly overcome, better and more balanced accounts continue to appear. We still await a scholarly English language campaign treatment from the Japanese perspective. It seems clear from the quotes in this essay that Japan understood Guadalcanal's nature from the beginning. Likely, the Japanese clearly understood their losses, while the Allies could only guess at them. The Western historical community can only hope that such will appear and lead to an even greater understanding of Guadalcanal and its central place in the story of the Second World War.

About the Author

William Lawson is a military historian and freelance writer. His academic focus is World War II, with an emphasis on American amphibious warfare. He earned his MA in American Military History, with a Graduate Certificate in World War II Studies, from American Military University. He is currently a Doctoral Candidate in History at Liberty University. He enjoys college football, collecting and shooting various firearms, and hanging out with his French Bulldogs Bilbo and Blueberry.

Endnotes

1 Richard B. Frank, *Guadalcanal: The Definitive Account of the Landmark Battle* (New York: Penguin Books, 1990), 613-614.

2 Samuel Eliot Morison, *The Struggle for Guadalcanal: Volume V of History of United States Naval Operations in World War II* (Boston: Little, Brown and Company, 1948), 372-373.

3   Samuel B. Griffith II, *The Battle for Guadalcanal* (Urbana and Chicago: University of Illinois Press, 1963), ix.

4   Robert Leckie, *Challenge for the Pacific: Guadalcanal: The Turning Point of the War* (New York: Bantam, 1965), ix-x.

5   John Toland, *The Rising Sun: The Decline and Fall of the Japanese Empire: 1936–1945* (New York: Random House, 1970), 431.

6   Ronald H. Spector, *Eagle Against the Sun: America's War with Japan* (New York: Vintage Books, 1985), 178, 218.

7   Frank, 617-618.

8   Jonathan Parshall and Anthony Tully, *Shattered Sword: The Untold Story of the Battle of Midway* (Washington, D.C.: Potomac Books, 2005), 422-423.

9   Jeter A. Isely and Philip A. Crowl, *The U.S. Marines and Amphibious War* (Princeton: Princeton University Press, 1951), 164-165.

10 Mark A. Stoler, *Allies and Adversaries, The Joint Chiefs of Staff, The Grand Alliance, and U.S. Strategy in World War II* (Chapel Hill: The University of North Carolina Press, 2000), 84-94.

11 Gerhard L Weinberg, *A World at Arms: A Global History of World War II* (Cambridge: Cambridge University Press, 1995), 344-348.

Bibliography

Cox, Jeffrey R., *Morning Star, Midnight Sun: The Early Guadalcanal-Solomons Campaign of World War II, August-October 1942*. Oxford: Osprey Publishing, 2018.

_____, *Blazing Star, Setting Sun: The Conclusion of the Guadalcanal-Solomons Campaign of World War II, November 1942-March 1943*. Oxford: Osprey Publishing, 2020.

Frank, Richard B., *Guadalcanal: The Definitive Account of the Landmark Battle*. New York: Penguin Books, 1992.

Griffith, Samuel B. II, *The Battle for Guadalcanal*. Urbana and Chicago: University of Illinois Press, 1963.

Hornfischer, James D., *Neptune's Inferno, The U.S. Navy at Guadalcanal*. New York, Bantam Books, 2011.

Hough, Frank O., Verle E. Ludwig, and Henry I. Shaw, Jr., *Pearl Harbor to Guadal-*

canal: History of US Marine Corps Operations in World War II, Volume I. Washington, D.C.: Historical Branch, G-3 Division, Headquarters, US Marine Corps, 1958.

Isely, Jeter A. and Crowl, Philip A., *The U.S. Marines and Amphibious War, Its Theory, and Its Practice in the Pacific.* Princeton: Princeton University Press, 1951.

Judge, Sean M., and Peter R. Mansoor. *The Turn of the Tide in the Pacific War: Strategic Initiative, Intelligence, and Command, 1941–1943.* Edited by House, Jonathan M. University Press of Kansas, 2018.

Leckie, Robert, *Helmet for My Pillow.* New York: Random House, 1957.

_____, *Challenge for the Pacific-Guadalcanal: The Turning Point of the War* New York: Bantam, 1965.

Merillat, Herbert, *The Island: A History of the First Marine Division on Guadalcanal.* New York: Houghton-Mifflin, 1944.

_____, *Guadalcanal Remembered.* New York: Dodd, Mead, 1982.

Miller, John, Jr., *Guadalcanal: The First Offensive, The United States Army in World War II: The War in the Pacific.* Washington, D.C.: US Army Center of Military History, 1949.

Miller, Thomas G., *The Cactus Air Force.* Fredericksburg, TX: The Admiral Nimitz Foundation, 1990. (Originally Published 1969).

Morison, Samuel Eliot, *The Struggle for Guadalcanal, August 1942-February 1943, Volume V of United States Naval Operations in World War II.* Boston: Little, Brown & Company, 1948.

Parshall, Jonathan and Anthony Tully, *Shattered Sword: The Untold Story of the Battle of Midway.* Washington, D.C.: Potomac Books, 2005.

Spector, Ronald H., *Eagle Against the Sun: The American War with Japan.* New York, Vintage Books, 1985.

Stoler, Mark A., *Allies and Adversaries, The Joint Chiefs of Staff, The Grand Alliance, and U.S. Strategy in World War II.* Chapel Hill: The University of North Carolina Press, 2000.

Toland, John, *The Rising Sun: The Decline and Fall of the Japanese Empire, 1936-1945.* New York: Random House, 1970.

Toll, Ian W., *The Conquering Tide: War in the Pacific Islands, 1942-1944.* New York: W.W. Norton & Company, 2015.

Tregaskis, Richard, *Guadalcanal Diary*. New York: Random House, 1943.

Twining, Merrill B. and Neil G. Carey, *No Bended Knee: The Battle for Guadalcanal: The Memoir of Gen. Merrill B. Twining USMC* (Ret.). Novato, CA: Presidio, 1996.

United States Navy, *The Landing in the Solomons, 7-8 August 1942*. Washington, D.C.: Publications Branch, Office of Naval Intelligence, 1943.

_____, *The Battle of Savo Island, 9 August 1942; The Battle of the Eastern Solomons, 23-25 August 1942*. Washington, D.C.: Publications Branch, Office of Naval Intelligence, 1943.

_____, *Battle of Cape Esperance, 11 October 1942; Battle of Santa Cruz Islands, 26 October 1942*. Washington, D.C.: Publications Branch, Office of Naval Intelligence, 1943.

_____, *Battle of Guadalcanal, 11-15 November 1942*. Washington, D.C.: Publications Branch, Office of Naval Intelligence, 1944.

_____, *Battle of Tassafaronga, 30 November 1942; Japanese Evacuation of Guadalcanal, Including the Loss of the* Chicago, *29 January-8 February 1943*. Washington, D.C.: Publications Branch, Office of Naval Intelligence, 1944.

Weinberg, Gerhard, *A World at Arms: A Global History of World War II*. Cambridge: Cambridge University Press, 1995.

Wheelan, Joseph, *Midnight in the Pacific: Guadalcanal-The World War II Battle that Turned the Tide of War*. Boston: Da Capo Press, 2017.

Not in Our Backyard: Soviet Incursions into Latin America and U.S. Responses during the Cold War

Christopher Booth

American Military University Alumni

Abstract

The Cold War was waged on a truly global scale, and Latin America was no exception as the bipolar competition between the United States and the Soviet Union indeed touched it. While it was often recognized as existing in the U.S. sphere of influence, there were several occasions when the Soviet Union attempted to increase its stature and sway in the region. Three examples stand out as the most significant, and those are the Soviet activities in Cuba, Chile, and Grenada. Each of these Soviet "incursions" into Latin America triggered an aggressive response from the United States. However, only one of the Soviet attempts to gain influence (Cuba) was processed in a serious manner by the USSR, while the other two were more passive. Consequently, the only attempt that had any lasting success for the Soviet Union was indeed their attempt to gain influence in Cuba.

Keywords: Cold War, Soviet Union, United States, Latin America, Chile, Cuba, Grenada, Intervention, Castro

No en nuestro patio trasero: incursiones soviéticas en América Latina y Respuestas de Estados Unidos durante la Guerra Fría

Resumen

La Guerra Fría se libró a una escala verdaderamente global, y América Latina no fue la excepción, ya que la competencia bipolar entre Estados Unidos y la Unión Soviética la tocó. Si bien a menudo se reconoció que existía en la esfera de influencia de los EE. UU., hubo varias ocasiones en las que la Unión Soviética intentó aumentar su estatura e influencia en la región. Tres ejemplos se destacan como los más significativos, y esos son las actividades soviéticas en Cuba, Chile y Granada. Cada una de estas "incursiones" soviéticas

doi: 10.18278/mhc.1.2.5

en América Latina desencadenó una respuesta agresiva de los Estados Unidos. Sin embargo, sólo uno de los intentos soviéticos de ganar influencia (Cuba) fue procesado de manera seria por la URSS, mientras que los otros dos fueron más pasivos. En consecuencia, el único intento que tuvo un éxito duradero para la Unión Soviética fue de hecho su intento de ganar influencia en Cuba.

Palabras clave: Guerra Fría, Unión Soviética, Estados Unidos, América Latina, Chile, Cuba, Granada, Intervención, Castro

别在我们的地盘：冷战期间苏联入侵拉丁美洲和美国对此的响应

摘要

冷战在全球范围内展开，拉美地区也不例外，因为美国和苏联之间的两极竞争确实影响了该地区。虽然拉美地区通常被认为处于美国的势力范围内，但苏联曾多次试图提高其在该地区的地位和影响力。最重要的三个例子是苏联在古巴、智利和格林纳达的活动。苏联对拉丁美洲的这三次"入侵"都引发了美国的强烈反应。然而，这三次活动中，只有在古巴进行的影响力尝试得到了苏联的严肃处理，而另外两次活动则较为被动。因此，苏联试图在古巴获得影响力的尝试是唯一一次取得持久成功的尝试。

关键词：冷战，苏联，美国，拉丁美洲，智利，古巴，格林纳达，干预，卡斯特罗

As much as World War II was a global conflict, the Cold War was arguably even more so as it touched lives and impacted governments on every continent. The battle between the United States and the Soviet Union was waged through proxy wars and intermediaries, from Asia to Africa to the Middle East. The international struggle for hegemony between the two countries would also be waged periodically in Latin America, which since the issuance of the Monroe Doctrine in 1823 and enforced as needed since then, had been considered by American leadership to be part of the U.S. sphere of influence. The Soviet Union indeed viewed Latin America during the Cold War as a difficult situation or with a "geographic fatalism" due to its own great distance from the area, the region's close proximity to the United States, the lack of an industrial proletariat of any consequence and the strength of the Catholic Church over the people.[1] However, all of those drawbacks did not prevent Soviet leadership from attempting to extend its reach into Latin America on several occasions during the Cold War.

It is a worthwhile endeavor to analyze the differences in three attempts by the Soviet Union to support socialist governments or increase its strength in Latin America, the de-facto American sphere of influence since President Monroe's famous doctrine of 1823. One of the three Soviet attempts was made in an aggressive manner, in Cuba in the early 1960s, which stands in stark contrast to the two other Soviet efforts, which were passive and led to underwhelming support of the democratically elected socialist government in Chile under Salvador Allende in the early 1970s and the newly formed socialist government on the island nation of Grenada in the early 1980s. All three of these efforts garnered great attention from American leadership, which worked actively and without reservation to repulse any Sovict gains in the region, and ultimately the Soviet Union would only achieve relative success in its endeavors in Cuba, which it processed in the most aggressive manner of the three.

The Cold War endured many ebbs and flows, leaders, and strategies. However, one aspect that remained firm was the U.S. commitment to combatting the spread, or even perceived spread, of socialism and corresponding Soviet power. American leaders instituted various methods to prevent the spread of what they deemed the antithesis of American values during the Cold War, but the primary underpinning of policy centered on containment. Promulgated by diplomat George F. Kennan (1904–2005), containment was essentially the prevention of the expansion of the Soviet Union and its influence by identifying areas of vital and peripheral interest and applying the appropriate amount of leverage dependent upon which distinction it received.[2] All three Soviet incursions mentioned earlier would be given vital status and treated accordingly by American leadership, who viewed any Soviet gains in Latin America as a direct loss for U.S. prestige and national security.

This approach by American leadership of acting to shape outcomes in the region to what the U.S. desired, often unilaterally, was perfectly in keeping with historical precedence. Early American leaders such as John Adams and his son, John Quincy Adams, viewed Latin America with deeply negative perspectives, and often saw these newly formed nations as countries that provided little value in a relationship with the United States and, thusly, desired to keep the U.S. as separate as possible from the region.[3] This mentality changed over time, and eventually the American presence in Latin America increased as the U.S. brokered trade deals, assisted with peace treaties and in general strengthened relationships. What did not change, however, was the view from Washington, D.C., that Latin America existed within the United States' sphere of influence, that European powers should not encroach into the region, and that the U.S. had the inherent right to dictate outcomes it wanted there. During the Cold War, American leadership would repeatedly use covert methods to influence regime change all across Latin America, ousting leaders it viewed as communist or even sympathetic to communists by using terrifying language to paint a scene of potential disaster if left uncorrected. The example of U.S. covert support to remove Guatemala's progressive leader Jacobo Arbenz in 1954 demonstrates this, as the overthrow was prefaced with talk of how "Guatemala is going to be a source of Red infection throughout Central America," rhetoric which encouraged the support of regime change and created powerful images of the horrifying scene if Guatemala was left to its own devices.[4]

With this perspective, it is easy to understand how the United States viewed Soviet incursion into Latin America as a significant threat to the stability of its national security and why it would work as hard as possible to ensure the Soviets did not gain traction in the region. The world had changed greatly from when America, under President Franklin Roosevelt, first officially recognized the Soviet Union in 1933, as he did so to normalize relations in the hope of combatting future enemies that he saw on the horizon (i.e., Nazi Germany).[5] In the post-World War II environment, the U.S. and Soviet Union worked to continuously improve

their own positions, and that is what the Soviet Union attempted in Latin America, first in Cuba in the early 1960s. Soviet involvement with the island nation would come after the Cuban revolution in 1959, a successful overthrow of the previously American supported Batista government by the guerilla movement led by Fidel Castro. It would not take long for Castro to rankle American perceptions with his bombastic discourse, but the situation only got worse as the Soviet Union began to support the new Castro led government which was becoming increasingly socialist in its actions and rhetoric.

The Soviet Union jumped aggressively at the chance to support what it viewed as a potential ally only 90 miles from the American mainland. In February 1960, it signed a $100 million dollar loan and sugar (Cuba's primary export) trade agreement with Cuba, and in May of that year formally established diplomatic relations. Acts like these further irritated American leadership under President Dwight Eisenhower, who had already tasked the Central Intelligence Agency (CIA) to investigate how to remove Castro.[6] Soviet leader Nikita Khrushchev also rallied behind Castro, publicly supporting him in international settings such as at the UN General Assembly, particularly after Castro began nationalizing American owned businesses throughout Cuba.[7] As Soviet relations strengthened with Cuba, American leadership resolved to take drastic measures to install a new government on the island that would be friendlier towards America. This would result in the CIA prepared invasion of anti-Castro forces at the Bay of Pigs in April of 1961, an attack easily thwarted by Castro's military.

The Bay of Pigs invasion directly spurred increased Soviet support of Cuba, which included the installation of intermediate range Soviet missiles on the island. This of course was intolerable to American leadership, and President John Kennedy demanded the Soviet removal of the missiles during the Cuban Missile Crisis of 1962. Khrushchev eventually agreed to American demands without consulting Castro, an act which infuriated Cuban leadership and momentarily soured the Soviet-Cuban relationship. However, that damage would only prove temporary, as the Soviet and Cuban alliance would continue until the end of the Cold War. While a majority of the Soviet support to Cuba was economic, there continued to be substantial military support inasmuch that Soviet assistance in that area would lead to Cuba becoming the world's second most militarized state per capita in the world.[8] Cuba continued to receive copious amounts of economic support, and in turn supported controversial Soviet decisions such as its 1968 invasion of Czechoslovakia and turning to Moscow instead of Beijing following the Sino-Soviet split.[9]

While the relationship was not always harmonious between the Soviet Union and Cuba during the Cold War (such as the Cuban supported efforts to spread socialism globally under revolutionary Che Guevara, something the Soviet Union did not endorse), it was largely a mutually beneficial relationship that Soviet leaders were willing to foster based if nothing else on the concern it drew from American leadership. Throughout the Cold War the Soviet Union would prop up Cuba's economy at great expense, as it and its Eastern Bloc allies absorbed about 85 percent of Cuban exports at prices well above market rate, along with supplying a number of products to Cuba at discounted rates or even as non-repayable grants.[10] The alliance was beneficial to the Soviet Union as Cuba could act where it could not, such as how it would receive assistance from Cuban military forces in Third World endeavors. This was evidenced when Cuban soldiers (which were estimated to number around 227,000 men in 1983) helped Soviet supported rebels attempt to seize control of the government in the African country of Angola.[11] Further, thousands of Cuban soldiers would help Soviet aims across the African continent in Ethiopia and Eritrea, as the Soviet Union attempted to sway outcomes of war there, but were heavily dependent on the 17,000 Cuban soldiers to directly impact the critical battles in those conflicts.[12]

This long-term association between the two countries regularly frustrated American leadership, but following the disaster of the Bay of Pigs invasion, President Lyndon Johnson decided to halt further attacks against Castro and opted to apply "containment" policies towards Cuba. These policies were intended to make life difficult for Cubans, to disaffect them towards Castro, and ultimately create a groundswell in the country for his removal.[13] American efforts in this area ensured that Cuba would remain dependent on the Soviet Union for key industries such as energy, as the USSR supplied almost 98% of Cuba's energy imports.[14] Furthermore, these economic actions were in line with previous Kennedy led decisions to encourage other Latin American leaders to break diplomatic ties with Cuba and assist in "strangling Cuba's economy" in return for Alliance for Progress initiatives.[15] While not effective at breaking the Cuban-Soviet alliance, American efforts to thwart Cuban success and growth were concerted and committed, and served as a strong counter to the continued Soviet support it received during this era.

The dedicated support the Soviet Union provided to Cuba during the Cold War contrasts sharply with how it interacted with the socialist government of Salvador Allende in Chile, who in 1970 became the first democratically elected Marxist head of state in the world. Overall, Soviet support of Allende was minimal and Moscow's approach to Chile during the early 1970s was very passive, and seemingly reluctant to upset the existing détente that existed between the USSR and the U.S. at that time. The Soviet Union largely viewed operations in Chile with an even more pronounced version of "geographic fatalism" than it did with regards to Cuba. Chile, being in the Southern Cone region of South America and much closer to Antarctica than the United States, provided the Soviet Union with little geopolitical value. What it did provide was the opportunity to again poke holes in American hegemony in its sphere of influence, made even more desirable by

the fact that Chile was one of the largest recipients of aid from the Alliance for Progress (17 billion dollars).[16]

That reasoning is why the Soviet Union provided what support it did to Chile and Allende, but the USSR assuredly did so to a much less substantial degree than what they provided to Cuba only a handful of years prior. The Soviet Union indeed provided funding to help finance Allende's earlier presidential campaign attempts, along with at least $400,000 in support of his victorious effort in 1970.[17] Once in office, Soviet officials attempted to strengthen ties via formal linkage through ambassadorial networks and through occasional, but small, funding grants. This minimal support would wane and disappear as Allende's grasp on power in Chile weakened before the coup that saw his death and the installation of a military junta under General Agosto Pinochet in 1973. Militarily this was demonstrated in the canceling of a Soviet arms shipment to Chile which was already underway, but was ordered to divert from its intended port in Chile and the weapons sold elsewhere.[18] The Soviet Union averred from wholeheartedly supporting the Chilean socialist government as well, as it roundly denied the approaches it received from Allende to increase trade from approximately $5 million in 1971 to $300 million in 1975, while providing Chile with desperately needed hard currency based on friendly trade agreements.[19]

Conversely, where the Soviet Union refused to secure the socialist Allende government in Chile, the United States was deeply devoted to seeing

North and South America

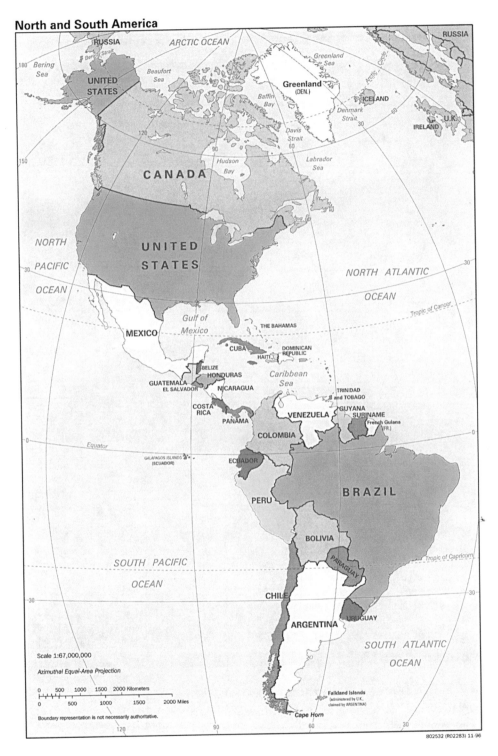

Image 1: Map of the Americas [The University of Texas Libraries, Perry-Castañeda Library Map Collection, Maps of the Americas, North and South America (Political), 1996.]

Image 2: Fidel Castro and Nikita Khrushchev make their way in the midst of a crowd. The close relationship between these two countries would frustrate U.S. leadership throughout the Cold War. [World Telegram & Sun photo by Herman Hiller, Library of Congress.]

its overthrow. The United States actively committed great sums of money to prevent Allende from electoral success, with reports of the CIA spending approximately $1 million dollars in a failed "spoiling campaign" in the lead up to the 1970 election.[20] Infuriated by the failed CIA attempts to keep Allende from power, American President Richard Nixon and his National Security Advisor Henry Kissinger vowed to keep pressure applied to Chile in the hope of inspiring a revolution that would see the socialist government removed from power. The U.S. coordinated this through its economic muscle in what would be nicknamed the "invisible blockade," where the U.S. National Security Council instructed two large aid agencies, the Export-Import Bank and the Agency for International Development to cease new commitments with Chile shortly after Allende's inauguration. This was followed by the Inter-American Development Bank refusing future loans and the World Bank suspending over $21 million dollars of agriculture loans to Chile, all due to U.S. pressure.[21] The U.S. would also authorize a budget of $6.4 million to further covertly destabilize Chile and create a situation ripe for a coup, which would ultimately occur on September 11, 1973.[22]

The American commitment to assisting the downfall of the Allende regime in Chile stands in stark contrast to the coolness of the Soviet effort to increase its position there. The reason is due to perception, whereby the prevailing sentiment in Washington, D.C. was that Chile was of vital geopolitical interest. Respected Cold War historian John Gaddis argues further that a misconception existed among American leadership, in that it was believed that a monolithic communist organization controlled such breakthroughs like the Marxist government in Chile and that this "perceptual lag" encouraged them to act forcefully to prevent such advances which were obviously coordinated by Moscow.[23] This reaction was out of balance with the tepid support the Soviet Union actually provided Chile during this period, but which American leadership was concerned would lead to a "Red sandwich" between Havana, Cuba and Santiago, Chile, if allowed to proceed unchecked.[24] The American perception of the Soviet Union masterminding the growth of international socialism existed even when evidence pointed to it being a grassroots campaign led by local leaders. The final aspect of American involvement in Chile was its staying power, where it continued to commit vast sums of money to support Chile's right wing leadership following Allende's ouster in 1973. In an effort to ensure socialism (and the Soviet Union) never returned to Chile, the U.S. granted $48 million in commodity credits, $132 million in food grants, $30 million in housing assistance and $238 million in loans, all to shovel dirt on the Soviet efforts at expansion in the region that generally never truly existed, particularly in comparison to the Soviet commitment to Cuba.[25]

The third example of Soviet adventurism in Latin America was its tepid cultivation of a relationship with the tiny island nation of Grenada in the early 1980s. Officially, the Soviet Union established diplomatic relations in September 1979, only months after the New Jewel Movement (NJM) had taken power of the small Caribbean island. However, the relationship did not immediately take off, as interestingly enough Grenada first reached out to the United States for recognition and alignment. This was ultimately rejected, as the U.S. government denied invitations to open a consulate on the island and refused to offer any sort of economic assistance to the island nation in much needed infrastructure projects.[26] It should come as no surprise then that Grenadian leadership under Maurice Bishop turned to the other global superpower for support, and signed numerous agreements with the Soviet Union before his death in 1983.

During the years of this short-lived alliance, the Soviet Union and, to a greater extent, Cuba, utilized the island to create a base of operations and staging area for matcrel. The Soviet Union would further prove to benefit from its relationship with Grenada, as it not only gained another island foothold in Latin America, but it also received a staunch ally that voted in favor of Soviet initiatives at the United Nations—even controversial ones such as those related to the Soviet invasion of Afghanistan.[27] The Soviet Union did commit some soft touches during this period, such as how it posted a large number of officials on the island, 47 at one point, and named a four-star general as the ambassador to the island, all of which impressed upon outsiders that the Soviet Union was taking the relationship between

the two countries seriously.[28] And yet Soviet leadership never truly committed to Grenada as an ally despite the benefits it received and the potential that it contained, as the Soviet Union ultimately gave very little economically to Grenada and trusted its leadership very little.[29] The two trade agreements between the Soviet Union and Grenada were not binding, and the three military agreements that the Soviet Union made with Grenada amounted to a total of less than 20 million rubles, far less than what it provided to other revolutionary Third World countries that it more heartily supported.[30]

Similar to the Soviet Union's half-hearted support of Chile and the United States' devoted attempt to counter what it perceived as an overwhelming Soviet encroachment, the minute Soviet support to Grenada was countered by an overpowering American military response. Immediately upon learning of Soviet recognition and potential agreements between the Soviet Union and Grenada, American leadership took an aggressive stance in an attempt to sour it early. In January 1980, the region was devastated by Hurricane Allen, and while the U.S. provided relief to other Caribbean nations, it purposefully withheld aid to Grenada and further instructed the outgoing ambassador to the region to visit every other island nation except Grenada.[31] These diplomatic and aid rejections were the extent of American reactions towards Grenada during the tail end of the Carter administration which was focused on maintaining the Carter Doctrine, policy which was directed overseas in

Image 3: Image of U.S President Richard Nixon and National Security Advisor Henry Kissinger. Kissinger and Nixon implemented efforts to destabilize the socialist government of Chile's democratically elected Salvador Allende. [National Archives, White House Photo Office Collection, Nixon White House Photographs.]

the Persian Gulf, not the Caribbean.[32] This changed drastically during President Reagan's presidency; however, he authorized American military forces to invade the island in 1983, which had been presaged with copious amounts of rhetoric which equated Grenada as one of the "Evil Empire's" Caribbean outposts.[33] The invasion (codenamed Operation Urgent Fury) was nominally a coalition effort as it was supported by elements from the Organization for Eastern Caribbean States (OECS), but was in reality a U.S. joint services operation that led to the securing of the island and the capturing of a great amount of military materiel. Despite mixed reception domestically and overwhelming disapproval from international organizations such as the United Nations, President Reagan stood firm behind the invasion which effectively ended any Soviet support of Grenada from that point forward as he proudly stated: "I will never be sorry that I made the decision to help you," to an audience of almost 90,000 Grenadians in 1986.[34]

The examination of these three case studies highlights some key similarities in both actions and outcomes. First, it cannot be overlooked that the only major success that the Soviet Union achieved in any of these three

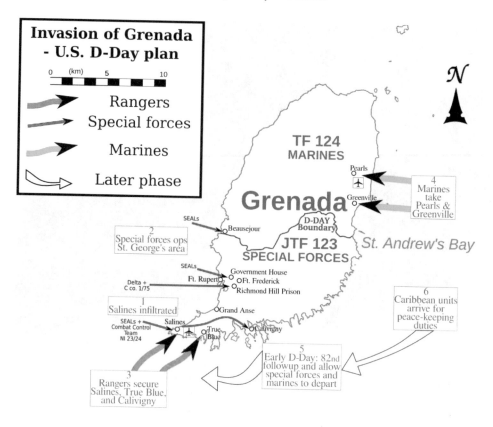

Image 4: Image of the proposed invasion plan of Grenada during Operation Urgent Fury. This joint effort revealed many inefficiencies with U.S. military operations but demonstrated President Ronald Reagan's commitment towards keeping Soviet influence out of the Western Hemisphere. [John M. Shalikashvili, Joint Chiefs of Staff, Wikimedia Commons.]

examples was in Cuba, which was the only instance that it processed relations with any sort of aggressive approach. In examining the two other examples where the Soviet Union processed relationships with Chile and Grenada in a more hesitant or less devoted manner, the Soviet Union gained nothing and was essentially removed from the country (in Chile by anti-communist Chilean government officials and in Grenada by the American military invasion). Conversely, through its decades long relationship with Cuba, the Soviet Union was able to maintain an ally with extremely close geographical proximity to the United States and one that, with Soviet economic assistance as an incentive, provided military support to desirable overseas initiatives along with backing of Soviet policies in the international arena.

The examples also demonstrate how the United States did not change its approach towards perceived Soviet incursions into Latin America. U.S. leadership abhorred the idea of rising Soviet influence in Latin America, and thusly combated such attempts with vigor in each instance. In Cuba, U.S. leadership launched a failed CIA led invasion to overthrow the Soviet supported leader, Fidel Castro. Once that failed, American leadership did not give up but instead increased economic pressure which would extend into a trade embargo that would eventually outlast the existence of the Soviet Union. In Chile, American leaders committed millions of dollars in efforts to prevent the Soviet supported politician Salvador Allende from winning the presidential election. After that operation failed, the U.S. government committed millions more to create economic imbalances and foster a state of existence that was conducive to a coup against Allende which would eventually see him overthrown. Finally, in Grenada, the U.S. refused aid and recognition in an attempt to sway the island nation back towards the West and away from Soviet influence, but after this resulted in less than desirable results, it launched a decisive military invasion which ensured there would be zero Soviet power left on the island.

The Soviet Union attempted on multiple occasions to increase its standing and influence in Latin America, which had been recognized as part of the U.S. sphere of influence. U.S. leadership considered Latin America a key aspect of its national security, and in turn, accepted no threats of incursion from the Soviet Union into Latin America lightly. During the Cold War the Soviet Union attempted three times to support relations with Latin American countries, once in an aggressive and concerted manner and twice in a more hesitant approach. Both of those latter attempts ended in failure, while the former registered a long-lasting alliance with a supportive socialist regime very close to American soil. However, the American response to all three attempts was the same: staunch, committed, and effective. The U.S. outspent Soviet attempts to support the socialist government in Chile under Salvador Allende and saw to his overthrow, while in Grenada the U.S. military conducted an invasion which led to the removal of all Soviet and Cuban footholds there. And while it was not successful in removing the Soviet Union from Cuba, the United States remained committed via economic pressures to ensure that Cuba did not rise to any prominence while allied with the USSR during the Cold War. While the policy of containment may have had complications in other areas of the world, it was definitely implemented effectively in Latin America, as U.S. leadership identified it as a vital zone and applied the maximum levers to ensure that the Soviet Union did not achieve predominance there during this period.

About the Author

Chris Booth holds a Bachelor of Arts degree in History from Georgia Southern University (2009), a Master of Arts degree in Military History from American Military University (2013), and a Master of Arts degree in Defense and Strategic Studies from the U.S. Naval War College (2023).

Bibliography

Crandall, Russell. *Gunboat Democracy: U.S. Interventions in the Dominican Republic, Grenada, and Panama.* New York: Rowman & Littlefield Publishers, Inc, 2006.

Fagen, Richard. "Cuba and the Soviet Union." *The Wilson Quarterly* 2, no. 1 (1976): 69–78.

Ferrer, Ada. *Cuba: An American History.* New York: Scribner Press, 2021.

Friedman, Norman. *The Fifty-Year War: Conflict and Strategy in the Cold War.* Annapolis: Naval Institute Press, 2000.

Gaddis, John. *On Grand Strategy.* New York: Penguin Press, 2018.

Gaddis, John. *Strategies of Containment: A Critical Appraisal of American National Security Policy during the Cold War.* Oxford: Oxford University Press, 2005.

Gaddis, John. *We Now Know: Rethinking Cold War History.* Oxford: Oxford University Press, 1997.

Garthoff, Raymond. *Détente and Confrontation: American-Soviet Relations from Nixon to Reagan.* Washington, D.C.: The Brookings Institution, 1985.

Gustafson, Kristian. *Hostile Intent: U.S. Covert Operations in Chile 1964–1974.* Washington D.C.: Potomac Books Inc., 2007.

Gustafson, K, & Andrew, C. "The other hidden hand: Soviet and Cuban intelligence in Allende's Chile." *Intelligence and National Security* 33, no. 3 (2018): 407–421.

Harmer, Tanya. *Allende's Chile & the Inter-American Cold War.* Chapel Hill: University of North Carolina Press, 2011.

Kinzer, Stephen. *Overthrow: America's Century of Regime Change from Hawaii to Iraq.* New York: Times Books, 2006.

Packenham, Robert A. "Cuba and the Soviet Union: What Kind of Dependency?" in *Cuban Communism* (6th Edition) Edited by Irving Louis Horowitz. Piscataway, NJ: Transaction Books, 1987.

Papp, Daniel. "The Soviet Union and Cuba in Ethiopia," *Current History 76*, no. 445 (1979): 110–30.

Rabe, Stephen. *The Killing Zone: The United States Wages Cold War in Latin America*. Oxford: Oxford University Press, 2015.

Schoultz, Lars. *Beneath the United States: A History of U.S. Policy toward Latin America*. Cambridge: Harvard University Press, 1998.

Shearman, Peter. "The Soviet Union and Grenada under the New Jewel Movement," *International Affairs 61*, no. 4 (1985): 661–674.

Westad, Odd Arne. *The Cold War: A World History*. New York: Basic Books, 2017.

Whelan, Joseph G. & Dixon, Michael J. *The Soviet Union in the Third World: Threat to World Peace?* Washington, D.C.: International Defense Publishers, Inc., 1986.

Yordanov, Radoslav. "Warsaw Pact Countries' Involvement in Chile from Frei to Pinochet, 1964-1973." *Journal of Cold War Studies 21*, no. 3 (2019): 56–87.

Zubok, Vladislav and Pleshakov, Constantine. *Inside the Kremlin's Cold War: From Stalin to Khruschev*. Cambridge: Harvard University Press, 1996.

Endnotes

1   John Gaddis, *We Now Know: Rethinking Cold War History* (Oxford: Oxford University Press, 1997), 177.

2   John Gaddis, *Strategies of Containment: A Critical Appraisal of American National Security Policy during the Cold War* (Oxford: Oxford University Press, 2005), 23.

3   Lars Schoultz, *Beneath the United States: A History of U.S. Policy toward Latin America* (Cambridge: Harvard University Press, 1998), 3–11.

4   Ibid., 339.

5   John Gaddis, *On Grand Strategy* (New York: Penguin Press, 2018), 280.

6   Richard Fagen, "Cuba and the Soviet Union," *The Wilson Quarterly 2*, no. 1 (1976): 70.

7   Vladislav Zubok and Constantine Pleshakov, *Inside the Kremlin's Cold War: From Sta-*

lin to Krushchev (Cambridge: Harvard University Press, 1996), 206–207.

8   Ada Ferrer, *Cuba: An American History* (New York: Scribner Press, 2021), 381.

9   Fagen, "Cuba and the Soviet Union," 74.

10 Ferrer, *Cuba: An American History*, 436.

11 Joseph Whelan, and Michael Dixon, *The Soviet Union in the Third World: Threat to World Peace?* (Washington, D.C.: International Defense Publishers, Inc., 1986): 311.

12 Daniel Papp, "The Soviet Union and Cuba in Ethiopia," *Current History 76*, no. 445 (1979): 113.

13 Stephen Rabe, *The Killing Zone: The United States Wages Cold War in Latin America* (Oxford: Oxford University Press, 2015), 80.

14 Robert A. Packenham, "Cuba and the Soviet Union: What Kind of Dependency? In *Cuban Communism* (6th Edition) Edited by Irving Louis Horowitz (Piscataway, NJ: Transaction Books, 1987), 147.

15 Rabe, *The Killing Zone*, 95.

16 Kristian Gustafson, and Christopher Andrew, "The other hidden hand: Soviet and Cuban intelligence in Allende's Chile," *Intelligence and National Security 33*, no. 3 (2018): 409.

17 Ibid., 410.

18 Radoslav Yordanov, "Warsaw Pact Countries' Involvement in Chile from Frei to Pinochet, 1964-1973." *Journal of Cold War Studies 21*, no. 3 (2019), 73–74.

19 Tanya Harmer, *Allende's Chile & the Inter-American Cold War* (Chapel Hill: University of North Carolina Press, 2011), 157–158.

20 Ibid., 48.

21 Stephen Kinzer, *Overthrow: America's Century of Regime Change from Hawaii to Iraq* (New York: Times Books, 2006), 185.

22 Kristian Gustafson, *Hostile Intent: U.S. Covert Operations in Chile 1964-1974* (Washington, D.C.: Potomac Books Inc., 2007), 160.

23 Gaddis, *Strategies of Containment*, 285.

24 Odd Arne Westad, *The Cold War: A World History* (New York: Basic Books, 2017), 356.

25 Rabe, *The Killing Zone*, 137.

26 Peter Shearman, "The Soviet Union and Grenada under the New Jewel Movement," *International Affairs 61*, no. 4 (1985): 662.

27 Ibid., 666.

28 Whelan and Dixon, *The Soviet Union in the Third World*, 341–342.

29 Raymond Garthoff, *Détente and Confrontation: American-Soviet Relations from Nixon to Reagan* (Washington, D.C.: The Brookings Institute, 1985), 1056.

30 Shearman, "The Soviet Union and Grenada," 669.

31 Russell Crandall, *Gunboat Democracy: U.S. Interventions in the Dominican Republic, Grenada, and Panama* (New York: Rowman & Littlefield Publishers Inc., 2006), 129.

32 Thomas Friedman, *The Fifty-Year War: Conflict and Strategy in the Cold War* (Annapolis: Naval Institute Press, 2000), 438.

33 Crandall, *Gunboat Democracy*, 106.

34 Ibid., 162.

Book Review: James Ellman's *MacArthur Reconsidered: General Douglas MacArthur as a Wartime Commander*

Dr. Robert Young

Associate Professor
Department of History and Military History
American Military University

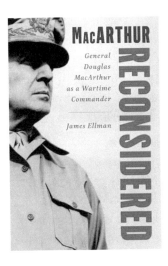

Ellman, James. *MacArthur Reconsidered: General Douglas MacArthur as a Wartime Commander.* Stackpole Books, Essex Connecticut, 2023. ISBN 9780811771560. Notes. Index. Bibliography. Pp. 276. Hardcover $29.95. Electronic version available.

James Ellman is a military history writer who has focused on World War II. He is the author of *Hitler's Greatest Gamble: A New Look at German Strategy, Operation Barbarossa, and the Axis Defeat in World War II* (2019). In *MacArthur Reconsidered: General Douglas MacArthur as a Wartime Commander*, Ellman evaluates the military record of the often criticized and sometimes praised general that saw his lengthy career terminated for insubordination. Though his early career, from graduating West Point to his assumption of the coveted position of Army Chief of Staff, is covered, most of this work is dedicated to the years he spent outside the United States, first as Military Advisor to the Governor of the Philippines, then as Commander of all American forces in those islands, and his World War II years. Ellman also extensively analyzes MacArthur's time in Japan from 1945–1950 and his conduct and decisions during the Korean War. This is a generally critical work although there are no signs of personal animosity. Ellman evaluates MacArthur in a fair and balanced manner.

The years preceding World War II and its first months demonstrated MacArthur's most pronounced failures and the true beginning of the self-de-

  doi: 10.18278/mhc.1.2.6

structive figure relieved for insubordination in 1951 by President Truman. As he was fleeing the Philippines early in World War II, MacArthur exclaimed, "I shall return!" Ellman does an excellent job of demonstrating MacArthur's culpability in the Philippines' fall to Japanese forces, being outgunned and outmanned in these early months. There is excellent background throughout the book, though his early chapter on the Philippines is the best. MacArthur misjudged both the capabilities and armament of his American and Filipino forces. In fact, Ellman asserts he blatantly lied when reporting the readiness of his command to Washington. He repeatedly told Washington that the Japanese would not attack the Philippines, as he would a decade later assure President Truman that the Chinese would not intervene in Korea (22). He took few measures to train his troops and, in the years immediately before World War II, two disturbing traits developed in MacArthur: his inability to take orders or direction from previous subordinates who were now superiors (Marshall in World War II and Bradley in Korea), and his detachment from frontline troops. Visits to forward commands were infrequent, and he never seemed to appreciate their trials and tribulations. Washington, however, was told of the strength of his command, and early strategy was undoubtedly influenced by the delusional reports they received (32). They believed, as MacArthur repeatedly stated, that he could defeat any force the Japanese launched against him.

Ellman is also critical of MacArthur's decision to essentially give most of Luzon to the Japanese and concentrate his forces in the Bataan Peninsula. Though he had shortages, the American Army on Luzon had adequate armor and artillery to repel a Japanese amphibious landing and/or severely damage them in a pitched battle. The stories of the supply-deprived American forces in the peninsula are true. What is not known to the general military history reader is that supplies did exist, and that they were stockpiled in Manila—knowingly abandoned when MacArthur decided to make his stand south of the city. Ellman's focus on the lesser known facts of his campaigns is perhaps his work's most outstanding achievement.

Ellman establishes patterns—not good ones—in MacArthur's campaigns. The years after World War II saw him as the quasi "Emperor" of Japan. He still commanded American occupation forces and was responsible for their training and readiness. When war broke out in Korea, they were neither trained nor ready. The situation was remarkably like the Philippines prior to World War II. MacArthur praised the readiness of his command to Washington, as he had done in the Philippines. He disparaged enemy capabilities, as he had done in the Philippines. Again, as with the Philippines, American forces were overwhelmed and embarrassed. Ellman gives proper praise to MacArthur for the daring gamble he took with an amphibious landing at Inchon. However, brilliance was followed by self-destructiveness. His inability to reign in his own opinions and insubordination towards superiors, in this case

President Truman, led to a dismissal a decade too late.

MacArthur enjoyed his greatest military successes during World War II, and the author quantifies those achievements. The New Guinea campaign, which history has lauded MacArthur for several brilliant decisions and maneuvers, resulted from a top-secret intelligence program, ULTRA, not just the general's so-called genius. Throughout the war, MacArthur seemed to lose interest in individual battles, declaring them "over" or "secure" while his troops continued to toil along in bitter fighting. Ellman once again points out that MacArthur rarely visited the front or saw the plight of his troops. However, he did return to the Philippines, and would have most likely commanded an invasion of Japan.

Throughout this work Ellman analyzes the individual as well as his war record. His insubordination is legendary. Along with that insubordination was an immense amount of disrespect. He spoke to and treated presidents as inferior, unworthy of him. Ordered to Washington to meet with President Roosevelt and the Joint Chiefs of Staff (JCS) to discuss Pacific strategy in 1944, he sent a few select staff members. He met FDR in Hawaii, keeping him waiting and lecturing him (120). He would not be denied. During the Korean War, President Truman had to come see him on Wake Island. The president was made to look like a subordinate, not the general's superior. Despite repeated orders to avoid contradictory statements on political or national strategic sub-

jects, he continued to publicly question Washington's decisions. Here, Ellman makes his most important assertion— MacArthur's superiors share responsibility for all he did because they did not control him when this behavior began.

Several times during World War II, MacArthur should have been relieved of his command. The author points to a conversation between President Roosevelt and journalist Edward R. Murrow after MacArthur's forces were caught unprepared in the Philippines. The Pearl Harbor commanders were removed from command and MacArthur should have suffered the same fate (43). He publicly questioned the U.S. strategy of "Germany first," causing FDR serious diplomatic problems with Stalin and Churchill. For that, he was not even reprimanded. Ellman lists many other transgressions for which he could have been relieved during the Second World War. During Korea, the press reported all his actions. During World War II they did not. The powers in Washington allowed MacArthur to grow bolder and bolder in his proclamations with nary a word. He called for an infusion of Nationalist Chinese troops from Formosa despite directives stating the president did not and dismissing the possibility of the war escalating. He questioned the decision to halt his forces, several times. But, as the author states, his "superiors in Washington abdicated their responsibility when the General chose to disobey orders" (146). When he disregarded a JCS directive on what they saw as a major problem in his force's dispositions, General Bradley, the JCS Chairman and his superior, commented "MacArthur treated us as if we were children" (208). Would any other American commander's behaving in such a manner be tolerated? When the Chinese intervened, MacArthur publicly stated he wanted to bomb Manchuria. Privately, President Truman felt he should have fired him then, but he did not, and when the inevitable finally happened, MacArthur was shocked and surprised (222). He had been allowed to do as he pleased for so long, why would he think anything would ever change?

MacArthur Reconsidered is an excellent addition to a military history library. Most MacArthur books cover one war or a specific time, but here you see the evolution of who William Manchester, MacArthur's most prominent biographer, called the "American Caesar." The book contains twenty pages of notes and an extensive bibliography. Ellman correctly points out the unreliability of most primary sources concerning MacArthur. They are basic puff pieces, done mostly under his personal supervision, extolling his "genius," and blatantly distorting the truth. The author may cause some to reassess their opinion of General of the Army Douglas MacArthur.

About The Author

Robert Young received a Ph.D. in Military History and Modern European Studies from the C.U.N.Y. Graduate Center in 2003, and a Master's in American History from Brooklyn College in 1994. He is currently an Associate Professor of History and Military History at American Military University. A veteran of the United States Army, he has served in various leadership positions in armored and cavalry units.

Book Review: *Bomb Group: The Eighth Air Force's 381st and the Allied Air Offensive Over Europe* by Paul Bingley and Mike Peters

Dr. Matt Meador

University of Tennessee at Martin

Bomb Group: The Eighth Air Force's 381st and the Allied Air Offensive Over Europe. By Paul Bingley and Mike Peters. Great Britain: Casemate Publishing, 2022. 406 pp. ISBN 978-1-61200-960-5

"The Mighty Eighth Air Force" during WWII is widely studied and written about. *Blood and Fears, Fear No More, The Mighty Eighth at War, With Wings of Eagles, 8th Air Force at War* are just a few titles recognizing an entire command through WWII, while other work available describes the war through first-hand accounts such as *The Boys in the B-17*, by T/Sgt James Hutchison. *Bomb Group: The Eighth Air Force's 381st and the Allied Air Offensive Over Europe* is a meticulously researched and comprehensive account of the experiences of one the "hottest" units of the U.S. Army Air Corps in European Theater Operations from 1943–1945, the 381st Bomb Group (BG). BG is written by Paul Bingley and Mike Peters, who both have extensive experience with

flight and the legacy of the 381st Bomb Group. Paul resides in the UK, draws on 30+ years of aviation experience, serves as the Chairman of the Ridgewell Commemorative Museum, and delivers presentations and hosts conversations about the airfield and unit history. Mike is a military historian, lives in the U.S., retired after 30 years of service in the Army Air Corps, and spends time writing histories and visiting airfields of units of "The Mighty Eighth."

Bingley and Peters created an in-depth glimpse at the lives of the enlisted men and officers who served in the 381st BG with a level of illustration and vividness that raises the bar on WWII unit histories, but by and large, the blending of first-hand accounts of the war. BG's chapter layout is linear in that readers experience the end-to-end life cycle

doi: 10.18278/mhc.1.2.7

of a single unit's creation, its training phases within the U.S. in 1942, shifting to combat missions over European targets from 1943 to 1945 while based at Royal Air Force (RAF) Ridgewell, and ends with the deactivation and discharge for many after the transfer of unit command and bombing operations in Europe stopped. Bingley and Peters devised chapters that are themed and differentiated by dates. For example, Chapter Three is "Big Leagues, 3 June 1943 – 14 July 1943" (16), which bounds readers to timeframes from chapter to chapter.

In each chapter, Bingley and Peters detail the lives of the men on the ground, whether sick or injured, in-between missions, experiences during air operations, and the return flights back to Ridgewell after missions were completed. Additionally, this work captured the emotions during these lived experiences of the men throughout. In one instance, as mission locations were identified, Chaplain Brown was present. For example, when Berlin, "Big B," was identified as a mission target, one airman looked to Chaplain Brown and said, "Keep on your knees all the time today (125)." The calmness of these statements knowing that the defensive network around Germany was a reality for the pilots and crews and put to action spiritual filters to ask for prayers of safety, are littered throughout the work. Additionally, while there are significant personal accounts of what the airman experienced, it should be mentioned that the chapters detail the lives of the airships of the 381st. Chapter Thirteen, Trafalgar, February 16–25, 1944, states

that B-17 "*Bermonsday Battler* didn't return … Five other B-17s had also been lost, another 50 men gone with them (169)."

Throughout the book, Bingley and Peters wove in Intermissions, providing a more profound and fuller context to the larger air war the 381st was involved in by discussing topics, such as airfields, strategic decisions that led to bombing campaigns and the impact on the war effort, and other informative snippets of the evolution of the B-17 aircraft in general (73-74). Bingley and Peters inserted a brief photo section creating opportunities to see the men and the aircraft of the unit; also included in BG is a glossary of acronyms, hierarchy of structure, and list of missions to include small details, such as aircraft loss, thus creating a better data-informed appendix experience.

Bingley and Peters drew from a wide range of sources to construct this book, such as military records, published and unpublished personal diaries, and letters, providing readers with a comprehensive and detailed account of the group's activities from 1943–1945. This allows readers to experience a unique WWII flying unit history. Chaplain Brown's *The Mighty Men of the 381st* was heavily cited throughout BG, but there are instances of using unpublished work by Brown, such as *Cup of Tea*. As mentioned, a significant amount of research went into the writing BG. Bingley and Peters left no stone unturned in their quest to capture the experiences of those serving in the 381st Bomb Group.

The richness of the experiences in the unit comes to life through anxiety, doubt, fear, loss, spirituality, worry, and triumph as the unit's time at Ridgewell. Readers are so close to what happened to the unit's men that it is as if they were right there with them. BG includes graphic accounts of the 381st Chaplain, James Good Brown. Chaplain Brown's war experiences are interwoven with the day-to-day lives of American flyers of the 381st. In Brown's writing, the chilling effects of the war became a reality when he states, "you look for faces and they are not there (54)." Additionally, Bingley and Peters also highlight the heartache of Chaplain Brown at the loss of every single unit member, and on several occasions, Brown was impacted mentally and physically due to the loss of members he had gotten close with (54). Bomb Group also piques curiosity about a side to the air war that remains largely uncharted: spiritual formation and counseling in bomber command. One recommendation to enhance the reading experience is the inclusion of a series of maps marking the point of origin at Ridgewell to a series of payload delivery locations as a way for readers to orient themselves with locations that the unit was tasked with bombing. Maps are not provided in Bomb Group, but their addition in the appendix or select locations throughout the book would have instantly added readership value.

Bomb Group concludes with a moving tribute to the members who served in the 381st, highlighting their bravery and sacrifices during the war. Bomb Group provides a glossary of acronyms to reference for understanding before the Appendix, but a note in the text directing readers to "see glossary on page 364" would have enhanced the experience versus stopping to read and search for the meaning of the acronyms. Furthermore, the photo collection consisted of unit aircraft, members, and operations, providing considerable depth to visualization of the 381st. Additionally, Bingley and Peters created an extensive bibliography connecting readers to an extensive body of knowledge and a list of curated web-based unit histories to extend research and reading opportunities to this one source should the opportunity be taken.

Bomb Group is a must-read for anyone interested in World War II history, aviation, or military strategy. If readers want to research a single unit's involvement in the air war over Europe, that requirement is met by reading through the covers of BG. By reading BG, those interested in religious studies may find the life of Chaplain Brown as fascinating as this author. For adding Chaplain Brown's experience elevated this book to another level.

About the Author

Matt Meador, Ed. D. is a Program Manager for FedEx in Memphis, TN. For the last fifteen years, Matt's central focus has been customer-driven design, development, implementation, and evaluation of training (project/program management) and performance platforms. As an adjunct history professor, Matt remains active in the educational and history community by teaching virtual and hybrid history courses for Southwest Tennessee Community College and UT Martin. Matt is currently writing several articles for the 2023–2024 calendar years intended for publication on higher education curriculum and instruction performance assessment, dimensional assessment and data interpretation, learning analytics as connecting the characteristics of a learning organization, and segments of Memphis regional history. Matt's research interests include the Learning Organization Framework Model, performance evaluation, leadership development, innovation studies beyond blended learning, and Memphis regional history. Matt has an off-duty supervisor of thirteen years and five children.

Veteran Profile: Sergeant Gim Chin United States Army – World War II

Alisha Hamel

American Military University

"The country has a long history of racial inequities. There were signs throughout California that were discriminatory against Chinamen. Military policy reflected public policy resulting in implicit bias. Military policy started to take the lead in integration during and after World War II. Chinese started to be integrated into the military during World War II well before African American integration."[1]

"When the United States entered World War II, about 29,000 persons of Chinese ancestry were living in Hawaii and another 78,000 on the mainland. By war's end, over 13,000 were serving in all branches of the Army Ground Forces and Army Air Forces.[2] Anti-Chinese sentiments in the U.S. were a constant reminder that Americans saw them as different and excluded them. Some enlisted, and some died, before the Chinese Exclusion Act of 1882 was finally repealed in December 1943…. The Chinese Americans who served in World War II represented about 25% of the Chinese population in America. This was the highest percentage of service for any American ethnic community in World War II."[3]

Gim Chin was interviewed on May 2, 2011, by Alisha Hamel at his home in San Francisco. Here is his firsthand account of his time in the U.S. Army during World War II.

"I joined the Army on February 25, 1941, and accidentally ended up in the Oregon National Guard. I wanted to be in the active-duty Army so I could be sent immediately to fight the Japanese in China. The Japanese had invaded China, and we saw on the news what they did in Nanking. It was terrible. The Rape of Nanking really affected me. Much to my surprise, when I showed up to my first drill with my National Guard unit, there were two Japanese-American Soldiers already in it. They quietly disappeared from my unit after the Japanese attack at Pearl Harbor. After December 7, 1941, the authorities rounded up all the Japanese in Portland and sent them to camps. I don't know where the two Japanese that had been in my unit went."

After the attack at Pearl Harbor,

doi: 10.18278/mhc.1.2.8

1941 company photo of L Company, 162ⁿᵈ Regiment, 41ˢᵗ Infantry Division, Oregon National Guard at Camp Murray next to Fort Lewis in Washington. Gim Chin is pictured in the center. He was the only Chinese American in his unit. (photographed from the personal collection of Gim Chin by Alisha Hamel)

there was panic along the west coast of the United States, with a strong feeling that the Japanese would continue from Hawaii to the west coast of the United States. U.S. troops were hastily sent to guard the coastline, and all Japanese Americans were under suspicion of possible espionage. The United States issued Executive Order 9066 of February 19, 1942, to allow all Japanese Americans to be rounded up and sent to relocation camps. Over 120,000 Japanese Americans from Oregon, Washington, and California endured relocation. Most removed lost homes and livelihoods.[4]

"I ended up in L Company of the Oregon National Guard. In September 1940, my unit was sent as part of the 41ˢᵗ Division to Fort Lewis to train. After the attack on Pearl Harbor, the 41ˢᵗ Infantry Division was shipped to Australia, where we were scheduled to receive additional jungle training. My unit sailed out of San Francisco on the USS Matsonia. When we got out to sea, I became seasick. While I was sick, someone sabotaged my gun by putting seawater in the barrel, which caused it to rust. After I started feeling better, I went to clean the rust from my weapon. As I was cleaning it, the L Company commander walked up to me. I

didn't see him, so I didn't salute him."

"The L Company commander had a racial problem and did not like the Chinese, so when I did not salute him, he put me in for a court martial. When the court martial went to the battalion commander, he brought me in and asked me these two questions, 'Did you fight with somebody?' I said, 'no.' 'Did you go AWOL?' I said, 'no.' The battalion commander then brought my company commander into his office and told him that not saluting an officer was not serious enough for a court martial. The battalion commander then pulled me out of L Company and assigned me to the battalion headquarters unit."

"My new job at battalion headquarters was to be the battalion commander's bodyguard. This was not a real

Gim Chin was photographed on the training ground between the barracks built at Camp Murray to house the troops of the 41st Infantry Division. The 41st Infantry Division was a National Guard infantry division that was activated to federal service and sent to Camp Murray, located next to Fort Lewis in Washington, on September 16, 1940, to prepare for the possibility of war prior to the American entrance into World War II. Initially, the division slept in tents, but barracks were built while they were there. (photographed from the personal collection of Gim Chin by Alisha Hamel)

Once the 41st Infantry Division arrived in Australia, the first American infantry division to arrive in Australia, Gim Chin was pulled from his unit and assigned to General Douglas MacArthur's security detail. Sergeant Gim Chin regularly walked patrol outside of General MacArthur's headquarters and had the opportunity to talk to General MacArthur. "He was a nice man. I forgot to salute him once, and he did not get me in trouble." (photographed from the personal collection of Gim Chin by Alisha Hamel)

job, but the battalion commander made it one. It saved my life. Even though the battalion commander said I was his bodyguard, he was actually my bodyguard. My battalion commander saved my life. Everyone called me the Colonel's boy. The battalion commander was a Lieutenant Colonel when I first met him, and his name was Maison, Harold Maison. While I worked for him, he was *promoted to colonel, but he still worried about me all the time. I was only paid $21 a month, but he gave me another $5 a month. He treated me like his own son. I owe Colonel Maison my life. He eventually became a general. The colonel was worried because he knew that his men thought that I looked Japanese, and he was afraid that they might shoot me. Everyone knew that my company com-*

General Douglas MacArthur, the commander of the Allied forces in the South-west Pacific Theater, was regularly driven to where his troops trained and fought. This is a photo of General MacArthur overlooking his troops during a training exercise. Sergeant Gim Chin was assigned to his security detail from 1942 to 1945. (photographed from the personal collection of Gim Chin by Alisha Hamel)

During World War II, General Douglas MacArthur was assigned a security detail to guard his headquarters at Menzies Hotel in Melbourne, Australia. The detail was assigned to the 813th MP Company, and two MPs were constantly on guard at the door to Menzies. In October 1942, MacArthur moved his headquarters to Brisbane on the northern coast of Australia - http://generalmacarthurs honorguard.com/wordpress/the-stories/the-stories-only-the-finest *mander had been planning to make sure that I did not survive very long once we went into combat."*

"After we got to Australia, I was sent to be on General MacArthur's security detail, so I did not see any fighting, though I did escort MacArthur onto the beach at Leyte, The Philippines where he stated that he had 'Returned.' I was sent to MacArthur in March of 1943 and was with MacArthur until after the war ended. I was discharged at Fort Lewis."

"General MacArthur was a long way from the front lines. At headquarters, we were on for four hours and off for eight hours. During our time off, we went into the nearest native village to see what was there. One time, I saw a turtle that was so big a lady was sitting on it."

During my guard shift, I walked on the outside of the wire surrounding General MacArthur's compound. Every morning, for about half an hour, General MacArthur walked on the inside of the wire, and I walked on the outside of the wire. Quite often, he talked to me through the wire. I was there to protect him. He was pretty good. One time I forgot to give him a salute. He never punished me."

MacArthur opened his headquarters in Tacloban on Leyte in October 1944. It was a big deal, symbolizing his return to the Philippines. Before that, his headquarters was in Hollandia on New Guinea, which he opened in May 1944 and used as a nerve center for many months. His rear detachment stayed in Hollandia when he went to Leyte and later joined MacArthur in Leyte.[5]

"When General MacArthur's headquarters moved to the Philippines, one of my buddies took my place to look for a new site for the headquarters. As he was driving around, he ran over a landmine and was killed. He was a good friend of mine. He had wanted me to come back to Virginia with him after the war. His dad was the Chief of Police in the town where he was from, and we were planning to be policemen together. He took my place to look for the new site because I had dysentery and had been flown to the hospital. My buddy was a good man and a good friend."

"I did see some American prisoners from the Japanese prison camps. They were in terrible condition because the Japanese had starved them. It made me sick. The Americans treated the Japanese prisoners well. We gave them food and shelter. After the war, I came back to the United States and had a good life."

Gim was born Hom Gim Hor in Toisan, China on January 31, 1916, and immigrated to the United States in the 1930s, crossing the Pacific on a boat to Seattle, Washington. Experiencing seasickness on his journey caused him to dislike boats for the rest of his life. He worked at his father's Chinese laundry and at a Chinese restaurant in Butte, Montana, while going to school with younger children to learn English.

Hearing about the Japanese invasion of China, he enlisted in the United States Army on Feb. 25, 1941. He trained at Fort Lewis near Seattle before deploying to the Pacific Theater with the 41st Division, 186th Infantry Regiment, 3rd Battalion. He participated in Pap-

General Harold G. Maison, pictured here as a captain, from his photo in the 1939 Oregon National Guard yearbook became a Lieutenant Colonel and Gim Chin's battalion commander when the 41st Infantry Division was activated for World War II. He most likely "saved" Gim Chin's life because Gim Chin's company commander was heard to say that Gim Chin was not going to survive his first encounter with the Japanese. Colonel Maison transferred Gim Chin from his infantry company to General MacArthur's security detail where he served from 1942-1945. Prior to World War II, Harold Maison was instrumental in creating the Oregon State Police and served as its first Chief Clerk. After he returned from World War II, he served as the Second Superintendent of the Oregon State Police from 1946 to 1966.

uan, Luzon, New Guinea, and Southern Philippines campaigns. Giving credit to Lt. Col. Harold Maison, Gim was selected and served as a guard to Gen. Douglas MacArthur and witnessed history when he escorted the General onto the shores of Leyte, Philippines. The arrival preceded the General's famous speech about liberating the Philippines. During Gim's military service, he earned the Distinguished Unit Badge, Good Conduct Medal, Asiatic-Pacific Service Medal, Philippine Liberation Medal with One Bronze Service Star,

and the American Defense Service Medal. He returned to the United States and was honorably discharged from the Army on June 30, 1945. He was a proud veteran and enjoyed reminiscing about his service.

Gim met his future wife, Margaret, while on leave in Sydney, Australia. Not having an actual date, but exchanging many letters, Margaret arrived in the United States, and the couple married on July 5, 1947, in San Francisco and began their family. Gim owned a restaurant in the Mission District and later a grocery store in Noe Valley. Gim and Margaret devoted their lives to their family and enjoyed raising their seven grandchildren during summer breaks and on weekends. The couple turned their kitchen into a short-order restaurant for their grandkids and often took them out for adventures across San Francisco.

Gim was a proud San Francisco 49ers fan and watched games each Sunday. Though he was a quiet man, he could often be heard shouting at the television during games. Gim tried to keep up with current events by reading the newspaper cover to cover and watching several news programs a day. He liked spending days at Bay Meadows Racecourse with a box of dim sum as he followed an elaborate system for picking winning horses. When at home, he listened to Chinese opera and classical music and watched comedy shows, such as *I Love Lucy, I Dream of Jeannie*, and *Bewitched*, and any films featuring Bob Hope, Bing Crosby, or John Wayne.

Gim Hor Chin, 97, passed away on Sunday, Jan. 20, 2013. He is survived by his children, Jennie Chin, Marilyn Chin, Karen Seddio, and Michael Chin, and his grandchildren, Melissa Navas, Serena Stagnaro, Margaret Navas, Thomas Chin, Christina Navas, James Seddio, and Kevin Navas. He was preceded in death by his wife, Margaret Chin. He is buried at Olivet Memorial Park in Colma, California.

About the Author

LTC (Ret.) Alisha Hamel is a 2017 graduate of the American Public University with a master's degree in military history with a focus on World War II. Her thesis was on Australian/American Relations during World War II, and she presented on that subject at the 2018 Society of Military Historians. In 2016, she co-wrote a book on Oregon military history and, in 2012, completed a documentary on the 41st Infantry Division during World War II, which played on Oregon Public Broadcasting and in many theaters throughout Oregon and Washington. She has written articles that have been published in the *Huffington Post, Army History Magazine*, and *The Saber and Scroll*. She has completed several additional short history films, including a 5-minute history of the Army for the Army Transportation Museum, where she was the director from 2018–2022. She is writing a book from her extensive World War II veteran oral histories collection. It is expected to be completed by June 2024.

Bibliography

Hampton II, Isaac W. "The Black Officer Corps" and "Conversations with Black Brass." A noted scholar of Social and Cultural African American Military History. Army Materiel Command Historian.

Hamel, Alisha. Oregon World War II Memorial Wall panel is located at the Capitol Mall in Salem, Oregon.

Kowalski, Chris. Pacific War historian and former MacArthur Memorial director.

Low, Russell, and Ricky Leo. "Brothers in Arms: Chinese American Soldiers Fought Heroically in WWII." AUSA Meetings & Events, 21 Apr. 2020, https://www.ausa.org/articles/brothers-arms-chinese-american-soldiers-fought-heroically-wwii.

McNaughton, James C. "Chinese-Americans in World War II." U.S. Army Center of Military History. Last modified May 16, 2000. https://history.army.mil/html/topics/apam/chinese-americans.html.

Endnotes

1   Dr. Isaac W. Hampton II, Army Materiel Command Historian. A noted scholar of Social and Cultural African American Military History. He is the author of "The Black Officer Corps" and "Conversations with Black Brass."

2   McNaughton, James C., "Chinese Americans in World War II." U.S. Army Center of Military History. Last modified May 16, 2000. https://history.army.mil/html/topics/apam/chinese-americans.html

3   Low, Russell, and Leo, Ricky, "Brothers in Arms: Chinese-American Soldiers Fought Heroically in WWII." AUSA Meetings & Events, 21 Apr. 2020, https://www.ausa.org/articles/brothers-arms-chinese-american-soldiers-fought-heroically-wwii

4   Alisha Hamel, Oregon World War II Memorial Wall panel located at the Capitol Mall in Salem, Oregon.

5   Chris Kowalski, Pacific War historian and former MacArthur Memorial director.

MILITARY HISTORY CHRONICLES
CALL FOR PAPERS—SUMMER 2024 CAMPAIGN

The *Military History Chronicles* is soliciting articles, books, and exhibition reviews for its Winter 2024 Campaign.

The theme of MHC is military history exclusively. All historical time periods and geographic regions are welcome, provided they address a topic of historical interest. Book, documentary film, or exhibition reviews should be on recent events, releases, or publications.

Students, alumni, faculty from all academic institutions, and unaffiliated independent scholars are welcome to submit their original work. This includes previously submitted and corrected coursework. In either case, submissions should not have been published elsewhere.

All submissions must adhere to the *Military History Chronicles'* submission guidelines which can be located at: https://saberandscroll. scholasticahq.com/for-authors.

The *Military History Chronicles* reserves the right to reject, without further review, any submissions that do not follow these guidelines or meet our high academic standards.

Any questions should be directed to Jeff Ballard, Editor-in-Chief, the *Military History Chronicles* at: EICatMHC@gmail.com.

--- **DEADLINES** ---

April 15, 2024: Working Title, Abstract (124 words max), and Keywords (8-12).

May 1, 2024: Full Manuscript

Policy Studies Organization Resources

The Policy Studies Organization (PSO) is a publisher of academic journals and books, sponsor of conferences, and producer of programs. There are numerous resources available for scholars, including:

Journals
Policy Studies Organization publishes dozens of journals on a range of topics:

Arts & International Affairs
Asian Politics & Policy
China Policy Journal
Digest of Middle East Studies
European Policy Analysis
Latin American Policy
Military History Chronicles
Popular Culture Review
Poverty & Public Policy
Proceedings of the PSO
Review of Policy Research
Risks, Hazards & Crisis in Public Policy
Ritual, Secrecy, & Civil Society
Saber & Scroll Historical Journal
Sculpture, Monuments, and Open Space (formerly Sculpture Review)
Sexuality, Gender & Policy
Security & Intelligence (formerly Global Security & Intelligence Studies)
Space Education and Strategic Applications
International Journal of Criminology
International Journal of Open Educational Resources
Journal on AI Policy and Complex Systems
Journal of Critical Infrastructure Policy
Journal of Indigenous Ways of Being, Knowing, and Doing
Journal of Online Learning Research and Practice

Indian Politics & Polity
Journal of Elder Studies
Policy & Internet
Policy Studies Journal
Policy Studies Yearbook
Politics & Policy
World Affairs
World Food Policy
World Medical & Health Policy
World Water Policy

Conferences
Policy Studies Organization hosts numerous conferences, including the Middle East Dialogue, Space Education and Strategic Applications, International Criminology Conference, Dupont Summit on Science, Technology and Environmental Policy, World Conference on Fraternalism, Freemasonry and History, AI – The Future of Education: Disruptive Teaching and Learning Models, Sport Management and Esport Conference, and the Internet Policy & Politics Conference. Recordings of these talks are available in the PSO Video Library.

Yearbook
The Policy Yearbook contains a detailed international listing of policy scholars with contact information, fields of specialization, research references, and an individual scholar's statements of research interests.

Curriculum Project
The Policy Studies Organization aims to provide resources for educators, policy makers, and community members, to promote the discussion and study of the various policies that affect our local and global society. Our curriculum project organizes PSO articles and other media by easily serachable themes.

For more information on these projects, access videos of past talks, and upcoming events, please visit us at:

ipsonet.org

Related Titles from Westphalia Press

The Limits of Moderation: Jimmy Carter and the Ironies of American Liberalism by Leo P. Ribuffo

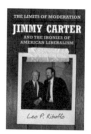

The Limits of Moderation: Jimmy Carter and the Ironies of American Liberalism is not a finished product. And yet, even in this unfinished stage, this book is a close and careful history of a short yet transformative period in American political history, when big changes were afoot.

The Zelensky Method by Grant Farred

Locating Russian's war within a global context, The Zelensky Method is unsparing in its critique of those nations, who have refused to condemn Russia's invasion and are doing everything they can to prevent economic sanctions from being imposed on the Kremlin.

Sinking into the Honey Trap: The Case of the Israeli-Palestinian Conflict by Daniel Bar-Tal, Barbara Doron, Translator

Sinking into the Honey Trap by Daniel Bar-Tal discusses how politics led Israel to advancing the occupation, and of the deterioration of democracy and morality that accelerates the growth of an authoritarian regime with nationalism and religiosity.

Notes From Flyover Country: An Atypical Life & Career by Max J. Skidmore

In this remarkable book, Skidmore discusses his "atypical life and career," and includes work from his long life in academe. Essays deal with the principles and creation of constitutions, anti-government attitudes, the influence of language usage on politics, and church-state relations.

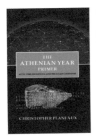

The Athenian Year Primer: Attic Time-Reckoning and the Julian Calendar
by Christopher Planeaux

The ability to translate ancient Athenian calendar references into precise Julian-Gregorian dates will not only assist Ancient Historians and Classicists to date numerous historical events with much greater accuracy but also aid epigraphists in the restorations of numerous Attic inscriptions.

Siddhartha: Life of the Buddha
by David L. Phillips,
contributions by Venerable Sitagu Sayadaw

Siddhartha: Life of the Buddha is an illustrated story for adults and children about the Buddha's birth, enlightenment and work for social justice. It includes illustrations from Pagan, Burma which are provided by Rev. Sitagu Sayadaw.

Growing Inequality: Bridging Complex Systems, Population Health, and Health Disparities
Editors: George A. Kaplan, Ana V. Diez Roux, Carl P. Simon, and Sandro Galea

Why is America's health is poorer than the health of other wealthy countries and why health inequities persist despite our efforts? In this book, researchers report on groundbreaking insights to simulate how these determinants come together to produce levels of population health and disparities and test new solutions.

Issues in Maritime Cyber Security
Edited by Dr. Joe DiRenzo III, Dr. Nicole K. Drumhiller, and Dr. Fred S. Roberts

The complexity of making MTS safe from cyber attack is daunting and the need for all stakeholders in both government (at all levels) and private industry to be involved in cyber security is more significant than ever as the use of the MTS continues to grow.

Female Emancipation and Masonic Membership: An Essential Collection
By Guillermo De Los Reyes Heredia

Female Emancipation and Masonic Membership: An Essential Combination is a collection of essays on Freemasonry and gender that promotes a transatlantic discussion of the study of the history of women and Freemasonry and their contribution in different countries.

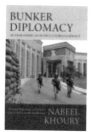

Bunker Diplomacy: An Arab-American in the U.S. Foreign Service
by Nabeel Khoury

After twenty-five years in the Foreign Service, Dr. Nabeel A. Khoury retired from the U.S. Department of State in 2013 with the rank of Minister Counselor. In his last overseas posting, Khoury served as deputy chief of mission at the U.S. embassy in Yemen (2004-2007).

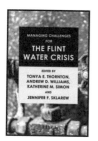

Managing Challenges for the Flint Water Crisis
Edited by Toyna E. Thornton, Andrew D. Williams, Katherine M. Simon, Jennifer F. Sklarew

This edited volume examines several public management and intergovernmental failures, with particular attention on social, political, and financial impacts. Understanding disaster meaning, even causality, is essential to the problem-solving process.

User-Centric Design
by Dr. Diane Stottlemyer

User-centric strategy can improve by using tools to manage performance using specific techniques. User-centric design is based on and centered around the users. They are an essential part of the design process and should have a say in what they want and need from the application based on behavior and performance.

Masonic Myths and Legends
by Pierre Mollier

Freemasonry is one of the few organizations whose teaching method is still based on symbols. It presents these symbols by inserting them into legends that are told to its members in initiation ceremonies. But its history itself has also given rise to a whole mythology.

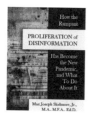

How the Rampant Proliferation of Disinformation has Become the New Pandemic by Max Joseph Skidmore Jr.

This work examines the causes of the overwhelming tidal wave of fake news, misinformation, disinformation, and propaganda, and the increase in information illiteracy and mistrust in higher education and traditional, vetted news outlets that make fact-checking a priority

Anti-Poverty Measures in America: Scientism and Other Obstacles
Editors, Max J. Skidmore and Biko Koenig

Anti-Poverty Measures in America brings together a remarkable collection of essays dealing with the inhibiting effects of scientism, an over-dependence on scientific methodology that is prevalent in the social sciences, and other obstacles to anti-poverty legislation.

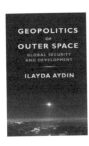

Geopolitics of Outer Space: Global Security and Development
by Ilayda Aydin

A desire for increased security and rapid development is driving nation-states to engage in an intensifying competition for the unique assets of space. This book analyses the Chinese-American space discourse from the lenses of international relations theory, history and political psychology to explore these questions.

Contests of Initiative: Countering China's Gray Zone Strategy in the East and South China Seas
by Dr. Raymond Kuo

China is engaged in a widespread assertion of sovereignty in the South and East China Seas. It employs a "gray zone" strategy: using coercive but sub-conventional military power to drive off challengers and prevent escalation, while simultaneously seizing territory and asserting maritime control.

Discourse of the Inquisitive
Editors: Jaclyn Maria Fowler and Bjorn Mercer

Good communication skills are necessary for articulating learning, especially in online classrooms. It is often through writing that learners demonstrate their ability to analyze and synthesize the new concepts presented in the classroom.

westphaliapress.org

Made in the USA
Columbia, SC
11 February 2024

31197947R00067